THE

FOURTH READER,

FOR

ADVANCED STUDENTS

BY WILLIAM H. McGUFFEY,
Professor in Miami University, Oxford

Editions 1836 – 1853

CINCINNATI:
PUBLISHED BY TRUMAN AND SMITH
150 MAIN STREET

ROMAN NUMERALS EXPLAINED

A numeral is a symbol meaning number. Our system of counting is believed to have begun by people counting on their fingers. Both the Arabic (1, 2, 3, 4, etc.) and the Roman (I, II, III, IV, etc.) are believed to have started this way. The word digit, meaning number, is from the Latin word digitus, meaning finger. The number V (5) seems to be representative of an open hand; the number X (10) seems to be like two open hands.

In earlier days, our forefathers used the Roman system to indicate chapter headings in books. To help you understand those numbers more easily you may refer to the chart below:

Roman	Arabic	Roman	Arabic	Roman	Arabic
I	1	XI	11	XXX	30
II	2	XII	12	XL	40
III	3	XIII	13	L	50
IV	4	XIV	14	LX	60
V	5	XV	15	LXX	70
VI	6	XVI	16	LXXX	80
VII	7	XVII	17	XC	90
VIII	8	XVIII	18	C	100
IX	9	XIX	19	D	500
X	10	XX	20	M	1000

Entered according to Act of Congress, in the year 1836
By TRUMAN & SMITH,
In the Clerk's Office for the District Court of Ohio.

The Moore–McGuffey Reader_TM is a trademark of Hewitt Research, Inc.

This edition copyright © 1983 by Moore Learning Systems, Box 9, Washougal, Washington 98671

Editors: Raymond S. Moore
Dorothy N. Moore
Jane Thayer

Cover illustration by Greg Constantine

ISBN 0-913717-04-5
Printed in the United States of America

PREFACE TO THE FOURTH READER

When William Holmes McGuffey's READERS debuted in 1836, one-room schoolhouses contained all eight grades, and students progressed at their individual rates. Therefore, it is important to remember that the FOURTH READER does not mean "a reader for the fourth grade." In fact, many reading authorities today say that some of the selections found in this volume are equivalent to reading material presented in today's high school and college classrooms.

In the preface to the 1838 edition, McGuffey addressed the question of reading level. He stated that the student of the FOURTH READER "is to expect that higher claims will be made upon his power of thought." In his 1853 preface, he said if any lessons are found "unintelligible" to the young readers, they will not be those lessons of the "highest character for thought." He explains: "Nothing is so difficult to be understood as nonsense. Nothing is so clear and easy to comprehend as the simplicity of wisdom."

In an early revision of the FOURTH READER, McGuffey added extensive instructions for oral reading and interpretation. Thirty pages of rules and explanations on topics such as articulation, tone, inflection, emphasis and pause prefaced the volume. Throughout the book, the rules were restated and reinforced with exercises. Although his methods may have been artificial, stilted or misapplied by teachers, speech authorities generally concede that McGuffey's instructions on oral reading served the purpose of standardizing American speech patterns—a task since taken over by radio and television.

As in the other volumes of the present edition, all new questions have been written for each lesson. A Spell-and-Define section has also been provided.

A unique feature of this edition of the FOURTH READER is the note preceding most lessons. Each note helps the reader understand the lesson's meaning, significance or historical setting. Information for the notes was researched from many sources, with particularly valuable material coming from THE ANNOTATED McGUFFEY: SELECTIONS FROM THE McGUFFEY ECLECTIC READERS, 1836–1920, by Stanley W. Lindberg (copyright © 1976 by Van Nostrand Reinhold Company; reprinted by permission of the publisher).

This volume completes the series of ECLECTIC READERS first written and compiled by William H. McGuffey. The first volumes contain elementary lessons dealing largely with problems of conduct. The last volumes introduce the advanced student to the "best of the forensic, descriptive, sacred, and poetic literature of the world," according to McGuffey authority H. C. Minnich. He wrote, "Young America was led into courts of justice, temples of worship, halls of legislatures, churchyards of illustrious dead, and was filled with emotions of heroism, of sacrifice, of sorrow, of patriotism and of noble living."

It is the hope of the present publishers that with this volume the young of a mature America will enter upon the same adventures.

—The Publishers

CONTENTS

LESSON I (1)

The Just Judge—ANONYMOUS

NOTE—The main character of this story is Sir Matthew Hale, Lord Chief Justice of England under Charles II and one of the most learned and capable lawyers in English legal history. As a judge, Hale made a remarkable impression on his contemporaries for his honesty, fairness, piety, and moderation.

A gentleman who possessed an estate worth about five hundred pounds a year, in the eastern part of England, had two sons. The eldest, being of a rambling disposition, went abroad. After several years his father died; the younger son, destroying his will, seized upon the estate. He announced that his elder brother was dead and bribed false witnesses to attest the truth of it.

In the course of time the older brother returned, but came home in destitute circumstances. His younger brother repulsed him with scorn and told him that he was an impostor and a cheat. He asserted that his real brother was dead long ago, and he could bring witnesses to prove it. The poor fellow, having neither money nor friends, was in a sad situation. He went around the parish making complaints and, at last, to a lawyer, who, when he had heard the poor man's story, replied, "You have nothing to give me. If I undertake your cause and lose it, it will bring me into disgrace, as all the wealth and evidence are on your brother's side.

"However, I will undertake it on this condition: you shall enter into an obligation to pay me one thousand guineas, if I gain the estate for you. If I lose it, I know the consequences; and I venture with my eyes open." Accordingly, he entered an action against the younger brother, which was to be tried at the next general assizes at Chelmsford in Essex.

The lawyer, having engaged in the cause of the young man, and being stimulated by the prospect of a thousand guineas, set his wits to work to contrive the best method to gain his end. At last he hit upon this happy thought: that he would consult the first judge of his age, Lord Chief Justice Hale. Accordingly, he hastened up to London and laid open the cause and all its circumstances. The judge, who was a great lover of justice, heard the case attentively and promised him all the assistance in his power.

The lawyer having taken leave, the judge contrived matters so as to finish all his business at the King's Bench before the assizes began at Chelmsford. When within a short distance of the place, he dismissed his servant and horses and sought a single house. He found one occupied by a miller. After some conversation, and making himself quite agreeable, he proposed to the miller to change *clothes* with him. As the judge had a very good suit on, the man had no reason to object.

Accordingly, the judge shifted from top to toe and put on a complete suit of the miller's best. Armed with a miller's hat and shoes and stick, he walked to Chelmsford and procured good lodging suitable for the assizes that should come on the next day. When the trials came on, he walked like an ignorant country fellow, backward and forward along the county hall. He observed narrowly what passed around him; and when the court began to fill, he found out the identity of the poor fellow who was the plaintiff.

As soon as he came into the hall, the miller drew up to him. "Honest friend," said he, "how is your cause like to go today?"

"Why, my cause is in a very precarious situation, and if I lose it, I am ruined for life."

"Well, honest friend," replied the miller, "will you take my advice? I will let you into a *secret*, which perhaps you do not know: every Englishman has the right and privilege to object to any one juryman out of the whole twelve. Now, you insist upon your privilege, without giving a reason why, and, if possible, get me chosen in his place, and I will do you all the service in my power."

Accordingly, when the clerk had called over the names of the jurymen, the plaintiff objected to one of them. The judge on the bench was offended with this liberty. "What do you mean," said he, "by objecting against *that* gentleman?"

"I mean, my lord, to assert my privilege as an Englishman, without giving a reason why."

The judge, who had been highly bribed by the younger brother, in order to conceal it by a show of candor and having a confidence in the superiority of his party, said, "Well, sir, as you claim your privilege in one instance, I will grant it. Whom in this room would you wish to have in that man's place?"

After a short time taken in consideration, "My lord," says he, "I wish to have an honest man chosen in." And looking around the court—"My lord, there is that miller in the court; we will have *him*, if you please." Accordingly, the miller was chosen in.

As soon as the clerk of the court had given them all their oaths, a little dextrous fellow came into the apartment and slipped ten golden guineas into the hands of eleven jurymen and gave the miller but five. He observed that they were all bribed as well as himself, and said to his next neighbor, in a soft whisper, "How much have *you* gotten?"

"Ten pieces," said he. But the miller concealed

what he had got himself. The cause was opened by the plaintiff's counsel. All the scraps of evidence they could pick up were adduced in his favor.

The younger brother was provided with a great number of witnesses and pleaders, all plentifully bribed, as well as the judge. The witnesses testified that they were in the self-same country when the brother died, and saw him buried. The counselors pleaded upon this accumulated evidence, and everything went with a full tide in favor of the younger brother. The judge summed up the evidence with great gravity and deliberation. "And now, gentlemen of the jury," said he, "lay your heads together and bring in your verdict as you shall deem most just."

They waited but for a few minutes before they determined in favor of the younger brother. The judge said, "Gentlemen, are you agreed? And who shall speak for you?"

"We are all agreed, my lord," replied one. "And our foreman shall speak for us."

"Hold, my lord," replied the miller, "we are *not* all agreed."

"Why?" said the judge in a very surly manner, "what's the matter with *you*? What reasons have *you* for disagreeing?"

"I have several reasons, my lord," replied the miller. "The first is, they have given to all these gentlemen of the jury, *ten* broad pieces of gold and to me only *five*, which you know is not fair. Besides, I have many objections to make to the false reasonings of the pleaders and the contradictory evidence of the witnesses."

Upon this, the miller began a discourse, which discovered such a vast penetration of judgment, such extensive knowledge of law, and was expressed with such manly and energetic eloquence, that it astonished the judge and the whole court.

As he was going on with his powerful demonstrations, the judge, in great surprise, stopped him. "Where did you come from, and who are you?"

"I came from Westminster Hall," replied the miller. "My name is Matthew Hale. I am Lord Chief Justice of the King's Bench. I have observed the iniquity of your proceedings this day. Therefore, come down from a seat which you are nowise worthy to hold. You are one of the corrupt parties in this iniquitous business. I will come up this moment and try the cause all over again."

Accordingly, Sir Matthew went up and with his miller's dress and hat on, began the trial from its very commencement, and searched every circumstance of truth and falsehood. He evinced the elder brother's title to the estate from the contradictory evidence of the witnesses and the false reasoning of the pleaders, unraveled all the sophistry to the very bottom, and gained a complete victory in favor of truth and justice.

QUESTIONS — 1. What were the circumstances under which the younger brother took possession of his father's estate? 2. How did he treat his elder brother upon his return? 3. What plan did Chief Justice Hall pursue? 4. What injustices in the courtroom did he uncover?

SPELL AND DEFINE — (1) disposition, seized; (2) destitute, impostor; (3) guineas, assizes; (6) ignorant, plaintiff; (8) precarious; (12) candor; (14) dextrous; (15) adduced; (16) verdict; (22) eloquence.

LESSON II (2)

Remarkable Preservation
PROF. WILSON

NOTE—As you read this story, remember that all sailing vessels mentioned in it were powered by and at the mercy of the wind.

You have often asked me to describe to you on paper an event in my life, which at the distance of thirty years, I cannot look back to without horror. No words can give an adequate image of the miseries I suffered during that fearful night, but I shall try to give you something like a faint shadow of them, that from it your soul may conceive what I must have suffered.

I was, you know, on my voyage back to my native country after an absence of five years spent in unintermitting toil in a foreign land to which I had been driven by a singular fatality. Our voyage had been most cheerful and prosperous, and on Christmas day we were within fifty leagues of port. Passengers and crew were all in the highest spirits, and the ship was alive with mirth and jollity.

The ship was sailing at the rate of seven knots an hour. A strong snowstorm blew, but steadily and without danger, and the ship kept boldly on her course, close reefed and mistress of the storm. While leaning over the gunwale, admiring the water rushing by like a foaming cataract, by some unaccountable accident, I lost my balance and in an instant fell overboard into the sea.

I remember a convulsive shuddering all over my

body and a hurried leaping of my heart as I felt myself about to lose hold of the vessel, and afterwards a sensation of the most icy chillness from immersion in the waves, but nothing resembling a fall or precipitation. When below the water, I think that a momentary belief rushed across my mind that the ship had suddenly sunk and that I was but one of a perishing crew. I imagined that I felt a hand with long fingers clutching at my legs and made violent efforts to escape, dragging after me as I thought, the body of some drowning wretch.

On rising to the surface, I recollected in a moment what had befallen me and uttered a cry of horror, which is in my ears to this day, and often makes me shudder, as if it were the mad shriek of another person in extremity of perilous agony. Often have I dreamed over again that dire moment and the cry I utter in my sleep is said to be something more horrible than a human voice. No ship was to be seen. She was gone forever.

The little happy world to which, a moment before, I had belonged, had been swept by, and I felt that God had flung me at once from the heart of joy, delight, and happiness into the uttermost abyss of mortal misery and despair. Yes! I felt that the Almighty God had done this—that there was an act, a fearful act of Providence, and miserable worm that I was, I thought that the act was cruel and a sort of wild, indefinite, objectless rage and wrath assailed me and took for awhile the place of that first shrieking terror. I gnashed my teeth and cursed myself—and, with bitter tears and yells, blasphemed the name of God.

It is true, my friend, that I did so. God forgave that wickedness. The Being, whom I then cursed, was, in His tender mercy, not unmindful of me—of me, a poor, blind, miserable, mistaken worm. But the waves dashed over me and struck me on the face and howled at me. The wind yelled and the snow beat like drifting sand into my eyes—and the ship, the *ship* was *gone*, and there was I left to struggle and buffet and gasp and sink and perish alone, unseen, and unpitied by man, and, as I thought too, by the everlasting God.

I tried to penetrate the surrounding darkness with my glaring eyes, that felt as if leaping from their sockets and saw, as if by miraculous power, to a great distance through the night—but no *ship*—nothing but white-crested waves and the dismal noise of thunder.

I shouted, shrieked, and yelled that I might be heard by the crew, till my voice was gone—and that too, when I knew that there were none to hear me. At last I became utterly speechless, and, when I tried to call aloud, there was nothing but a silent gasp and convulsion—while the waves came upon me like stunning blows, reiterated, and drove me along like a log of wood or a dead animal.

All this time I was not conscious of any act of swimming, but I soon found that I had instinctively been exerting all my power and skill, and both were requisite to keep me alive in the tumultuous wake of the ship. Something struck me harder than a wave. What it was I knew not, but I grasped it with a passionate violence, for the hope of salvation came suddenly over me, and with a sudden transition from despair, I felt that I was rescued.

I had the same thought as if I had been suddenly heaved on shore by a wave. The crew had thrown overboard everything they thought could afford me the slightest chance of escape from death, and a hen-coop had drifted towards me. At once all the stories I had ever read of mariners miraculously saved at sea, rushed across my recollection. I had an object to cling to, which I knew would enable me to prolong my existence.

I was no longer helpless on the cold weltering world of waters, and the thought that my friends were thinking of me and doing all they could for me, gave to me a wonderful courage. I may yet pass the night in the ship, I thought; and I looked around eagerly to hear the rush of her prow or to see through the snow the gleaming of her sails.

This was but a momentary gladness. The ship, I knew, could not be far off, but, for any good she could do me, she might as well have been in the heart of the Atlantic Ocean. Ere she could have altered her course, I must have drifted a long way to leeward, and in that dim snowy night how was such a speck to be seen? I saw a flash of lightning, and then there was thunder. It was the ship firing a gun to let me know, if still alive, that she was somewhere lying to.

But wherefore? I was separated from her by a dire necessity—by many thousand fierce waves that would not let my shrieks be heard. Each succeeding gun was heard fainter and fainter, until at last I cursed the sound, that, scarcely heard above the hollow rumbling of the tempestuous sea, told me that the ship was farther and farther off, until she and her heartless crew had left me to my fate.

Why did they not send out all their boats to row round and round all that night through, for the sake of one whom they pretended to love so well? I blamed, blessed, and cursed them by fits, till every emotion of my soul was exhausted, and I clung in sullen despair to the wretched piece of wood that still kept me from eternity.

Everything was now seen in its absolute dreadful reality. I was a castaway—no hope of rescue. It was broad daylight and the storm had ceased, but clouds lay round the horizon and no land was to be seen. What dreadful clouds! Some black as pitch and charged with thunder; others like cliffs of fire, and here and there all streamered over with blood. It was indeed a sullen, wrathful and despairing sky.

The sun itself was a dull brazen orb, cold, dead, and beamless. I beheld three ships afar off, but all their heads were turned away from me. For whole hours they would adhere motionless to the sea, while I drifted away from them; and then a rushing wind would spring up, and carry them, one by one, into the darkness of the stormy distance. Many birds came close to me, as if to flap me with their large spreading wings, screamed round and round me, and then flew away in their strength and beauty and happiness.

I now felt myself indeed dying. A calm came over me. I prayed devoutly for forgiveness of my sins and for all my friends on earth. A ringing was in my ears, and I remember only the hollow fluctuations of the sea with which I seemed to be blended, and a sinking down and down an unfathomable depth, which I thought was Death, and into the kingdom of the eternal Future.

I awoke from insensibility and oblivion with a hideous, racking pain in my head and loins, and in a place of utter darkness. I heard a voice say, "Praise the Lord." My agony was dreadful, and I cried aloud. Wan, glimmering, melancholy lights, kept moving to and fro. I heard dismal whisperings, and now and then a pale silent ghost glided by. A hideous din was overhead, and around me the fierce dashing of the waves. Was I in the land of spirits?

But, why strive to recount the mortal pain of my recovery, the soul-humbling gratitude that took possession of my being? I was lying in the cabin of a ship and kindly tended by a humane and skillful man. I had been picked up, apparently dead, and cold. The hand of God was there. Adieu, my dear friend. It is now the hour of rest, and I hasten to fall down on my knees before the merciful Being who took pity upon me and who, at the intercession of our Redeemer, may, I hope pardon all my sins.

QUESTIONS — 1. What was the Professor doing when his accident occurred? 2. Contrast the Professor's world on board ship and his world when he fell overboard. 3. What were his feelings when he first fell overboard? How did they change? 4. How did he escape a watery grave?

SPELL AND DEFINE — (1) adequate; (2) unintermitting, passengers; (3) moonlight, gunwale, unaccountable; (4) shuddering, immersion, precipitation, momentary, clutching; (6) uttermost, shrieking; (7) unmindful; (8) surrounding, miraculous; (10) instinctively; (11) overboard; (13) leeward; (14) tempestuous; (16) streamered; (18) fluctuations, unfathomed.

LESSON III (3)

The Maniac—ANONYMOUS

NOTE—A ducat is a coin of silver or gold first issued in the mid-1100's and called a *ducat* because it was issued by authority of a duchy. Later used in all southern European countries, the gold coins were valued between $1.46 and $2.32.

A gentleman who had traveled in Europe relates that he one day visited the hospital of Berlin, where he saw a man whose exterior was very striking. His figure, tall and commanding, was bending with age, but more with sorrow. The few scattered hairs which remained on his temples were white, almost as the driven snow, and the deepest melancholy was depicted in his countenance.

On inquiring who he was and what brought him there, he startled, as if from sleep, and after looking around him, began with slow and measured steps to stride the hall, repeating in a low but audible voice, "Once one is two; once one is two."

Now and then he would stop and remain with his arms folded on his breast, as if in contemplation, for some minutes. Then again resuming his walk, he continued to repeat, "Once one is two; once one is two." His story, as our traveler understood it, was as follows.

Conrad Lange, collector of the revenues of the city of Berlin, had long been known as a man whom nothing could divert from the paths of honesty. Scrupulously exacting in all his dealings, and assiduous in the discharge of his official duties, he had acquired the good will and esteem of all who knew him, and the confidence of the minister of finance, whose duty it is to inspect the accounts of all officers connected with the revenue.

On casting up his accounts at the close of a particular year, Mr. Lange found a *deficit* of ten thousand ducats. Alarmed at this discovery, he went to the minister, presented his accounts, and informed him that he did not know how it had arisen, and that he had been robbed by some person bent on his ruin.

The minister received his accounts, but thinking it a duty to secure a person who might probably be a defaulter, he caused Mr. Lange to be arrested, and put his accounts into the hands of one of his secretaries, for inspections, who returned them the day after, with the information that the deficiency arose from a miscalculation; that in multiplying, Mr. Lange had said, *once one is two*, instead of, once one is *one.*

The poor man was immediately released from confinement, his accounts returned, and the mistake pointed out. During his imprisonment, which lasted but two days, he had neither eaten, drunk, nor slept—and when he appeared, his countenance was as pale as death. On receiving his accounts, he was a long time silent; then suddenly awaking as if from a trance, he repeated, "once one is two."

He appeared to be entirely insensible of his situation; would neither eat nor drink, unless solicited; and took notice of nothing that passed around him. While repeating his accustomed phrase, if anyone corrected him by saying, "once one is *one*," he was recalled for a moment, and said, "Ah, right, once one *is* one." Then resuming his walk, he continued to repeat, "once one is two." He died shortly after the traveler left Berlin.

This affecting story, whether true or untrue, obviously abounds with lessons of instruction. Alas! how easily is the human mind thrown off its "balance," especially when it is stayed on *this world* only—and has no experimental knowledge of the meaning of the injunction of Scripture to cast all our cares upon Him who careth for us and who heareth even the young ravens when they cry.

QUESTIONS — 1. What had caused a deficit to appear in the city books of revenue? 2. Conrad Lange had a reputation as an honest man. Why did he "lose his mind" when his reputation was in question for only two days? 3. What responsibility for this tragedy must be shared by the minister of finance? 4. What alternative behavior does the author advise in his conclusion?

SPELL AND DEFINE — (1) hospital, commanding, melancholy; (2) measured; (3) contemplation, traveler; (4) assiduous, finance; (6) defaulter, secretaries, miscalculation, multiplying; (7) imprisonment; (8) solicited; (9) experimental.

LESSON IV (4)

True and False Philanthropy

Mr. Fantom: I despise a narrow field. O for the reign of universal benevolence! I want to make *all mankind* good and happy.

Mr. Goodman: Dear me! Sure, that must be a wholesale sort of a job. Had you not better try your hand at a *town* or *neighborhood* first?

Mr. F.: Sir, I have a plan in my head for relieving the miseries of the *whole world.* Everything is bad as it now stands. I would alter all the laws and put an end to all the wars in the world. I would put an end to all punishments. I would not leave a single prisoner on the face of the globe. *This* is what I call doing things on a grand scale.

Mr. G.: A scale with a vengeance! As to releasing the prisoners, however, I do not much like that, as it would be liberating a few rogues at the expense of all honest men, but as to the rest of your plan, if all countries would be so good as to turn *Christians*, it might be helped on a good deal. There would be still misery enough left indeed, because God intended this world should be earth and not heaven. But, sir, among all your changes, you must destroy human corruption before you can make the world quite as perfect as you pretend.

Mr. F.: Your project would *rivet* the chains which *mine* is designed to *break*.

Mr. G.: Sir, I have no projects. Projects are, in general, the offspring of restlessness, vanity, and idleness. I am too busy for projects, too contented for theories, and, I hope, have too much honesty and humility for a philosopher. The utmost extent of my ambition at present is, to redress the wrongs of a poor apprentice, who has been cruelly used by his master. Indeed, I have another little scheme, which is to prosecute a fellow, who has sent a poor wretch to the poorhouse to perish through neglect, and you must assist me.

Mr. F.: Let the town do that. You must not apply to me for the redress of such petty grievances. I own that the wrongs of the Poles and South Americans so fill my mind, as to leave me no time to attend to the petty sorrows of poorhouses and apprentices. It is provinces, empires, continents, that the benevolence of the philosopher embraces; everyone can do a little paltry good to his next neighbor.

Mr. G.: Everyone *can*, but I do not see that everyone *does*. If they would, indeed, your business would be ready done to your hands, and your grand ocean of benevolence would be filled with the drops which private charity would throw into it. I am glad, however, you are such a friend to the prisoners, because I am just now getting a little subscription to set free your poor old friend, Tom Saunders, a very honest brother mechanic, who first got into debt, and then into jail, through no fault of his own, but merely through the pressure of the times. A number of us have given a trifle every week toward maintaining his young family since he has been in prison, but we think we shall do much more service to Saunders, and indeed, in the end, lighten our own expense, by paying down all at once a little sum to release him and put him in the way of maintaining his family again. We have made up all the money except five dollars. I am already promised four, and you have nothing to do but to give me the fifth. And so, for a single dollar, without any of the trouble we have had in arranging the matter, you will, at once, have the pleasure of helping to save a worthy family from starving, of redeeming an old friend from jail, and of putting a little of your boasted benevolence into action. Realize! Mr. Fantom—there is nothing like realizing.

Mr. F.: Why, hark, Mr. Goodman, do not think I value a dollar. No sir, I despise money: it is trash, it is dirt, and beneath the regard of a wise man. It is one of the unfeeling inventions of artificial society. Sir, I could talk to you half a day on the abuse of riches and my own contempt of money.

Mr. G.: O pray do not give yourself that trouble. It will be a much easier way of proving your sincerity just to put your hand into your pocket and give me a dollar without saying a word about it. And then to you, who value *time* so *much*, and *money* so *little*, it will cut the matter short. But come now, (for I see you will give nothing), I should be mighty glad to know what is the sort of good you do yourself, since you always object to what is done by others.

Mr. F.: Sir, the object of a true philosopher is to diffuse light and knowledge. I wish to see the whole world enlightened.

Mr. G.: Well, Mr. Fantom, you are a wonderful man, to keep up such a stock of benevolence at so small an expense; to love mankind so dearly, and yet avoid all opportunities of doing them good; to have such a noble zeal for the millions, and to feel so little compassion for the units; to long to free empires and enlighten kingdoms, and deny instruction to your own village and comfort to your own family. Surely, none but a philosopher could indulge so much philanthropy and so much frugality at the same time. But come, do assist me in a partition I am making in our poorhouse, between the old, whom I want to have better fed, and the young, whom I want to have more worked.

Mr. F.: Sir, my mind is so engrossed with the partition of Poland that I cannot bring it down to an object of such insignificance. I despise the man, whose benevolence is swallowed up in the narrow concerns of his own family, or village, or country.

Mr. G.: Well, now I have a notion that it is as good to do one's own duty, as the duty of another man; and that to do good at *home*, is as important as to do good *abroad*. For my part, I would rather help Tom Saunders to freedom, as a Pole or a South American, though I should be very glad to help them, too. But one must begin to love somewhere, and to do good somewhere; and I think it is as natural to love one's own family and to do good in one's own neighborhood, as to anybody else. And if every man in every family, village, and county did the same, why then all the schemes would meet, and the end of one village or town where I was doing good, would be the beginning of another village where somebody else was doing good. So my schemes would jut into my neighbor's; his projects would unite with those of some other local reformer; and all would fit with a sort of dovetail exactness.

Mr. F.: Sir, a man of large views will be on the watch for great occasions to prove his benevolence.

Mr. G.: Yes, sir, but if they are so distant that he cannot reach them or so vast that he cannot grasp them, he may let a thousand little, snug, kind, good actions slip through his fingers in the meanwhile. And so, between the great things that he *cannot* do, and the little ones that he *will not* do, life passes, and *nothing* will be done.

QUESTIONS — 1. What do the names of the two characters in this dialogue tell you about the author's attitude toward each of them? 2. What does Mr. Goodman consider to be the root problem that must be corrected before the world can be made perfect? 3. If you wish to be useful, where must you begin? 4. Why do some people prefer grand schemes rather than small, simple ones? 5. How did Mr. Fantom prove his insincerity?

SPELL AND DEFINE — (1) universal; (3) miseries, punishments; (4) vengeance, prisoners; (6) restlessness, philosopher, wretch; (7) grievances, provinces; (8) business, charity, realize; (9) artificial; (10) sincerity; (11) diffuse, enlightened; (12) frugality, philanthropy.

LESSON V (5)

Scene at the Sandwich Islands
STEWART

NOTE—When the first Christian missionaries arrived in Hawaii (Sandwich Islands) in 1820, they set as their first tasks: learning the language, reducing it into a written form, and translating the Bible into the native language. Their first convert (1823) was Keopuolani, head queen of Kamehameha and mother of the next two kings. The following story is an eye-witness account of Christianity conquering heathenism.

At an early hour of the morning, even before we had taken our breakfast on board ship, a single islander here or there, or a group of three or four, wrapped in their large mantles of various hues, might be seen winding their way among the groves fringing the bay on the east or descending from the hills and ravine on the north towards the chapel. By degrees their numbers increased until, in a short time, every path along the beach and over the uplands presented an almost uninterrupted procession of both sexes and of every age, all pressing to the house of God.

So few canoes had been around the ship yesterday and the landing place had been so little thronged, as our boats passed to and fro, that one might have thought the district but thinly inhabited; but now, such multitudes were seen gathering from various directions, that the exclamation, "What crowds of people! What crowds of people!" was heard from the quarter-deck to the forecastle.

Even to myself it was a sight of surprise—surprise not at the magnitude of the population, but that the object for which they were evidently assembling should bring together so great a multitude. And as my thought re-echoed the words, "What crowds of people!" remembrances and affections of deep power came over me, and the silent musings of my heart were, "What a change—what a happy change!"

When at this very place, only four years ago, the known wishes and example of chiefs of high authority, the daily persuasion of teachers, added to motives of curiosity and novelty, could scarcely induce a hundred of the inhabitants to give an irregular, careless, and impatient attendance on the services of the sanctuary. But now,

"Like mountain torronto pouring to the main,
From every glen a living stream came forth—
From every hill, in crowds, they hastened down,
To worship Him, who deigns, in humblest fane,
On wildest shore, to meet th' upright in heart."

The scene, as looked on from our ship, in the stillness of a brightly-beaming Sabbath morning, was well calculated to prepare the mind for strong impressions on a nearer view, when the conclusion of our own public worship should allow us to go on shore. Mr. Goodrich had apprized us that he had found it expedient to hold both the services of the Sabbath in the forepart of the day, that all might have the benefit of two sermons and still reach their abodes before nightfall. For,

> "Numbers dwelt remote,
> And first must traverse many a weary mile,
> To reach the altar of the God they love."

It was about 12 o'clock when we went on shore— the captain and first lieutenant, the purser, surgeon, several of the midshipmen, and myself. Though the services had commenced when we landed, large numbers were seen circling the doors without, but, as we afterwards found, only from the impracticability of obtaining places within.

The house is an immense structure, capable of containing many thousands, every part of which was filled, except a small area in front of the pulpit where seats were reserved for us and to which we made our way in slow and tedious procession from the difficulty of finding a spot to place even our footsteps, without treading on limbs of the people, seated on their feet as closely, almost, as they could be stowed.

As we entered, Mr. Goodrich paused in his sermon, till we should be seated. I ascended the pulpit beside him, from which I had a full view of the congregation. The suspense of attention in the people was only momentary, notwithstanding the entire novelty to them of the laced coats, cocked hats, and other appendages of naval uniform. I can scarce describe the emotions experienced in glancing an eye over the immense number, seated so thickly on the matted floor as to seem literally one mass of heads, covering an area of more than nine thousand square feet. The sight was most striking, and soon became, not only to myself, but to some of my fellow officers, deeply affecting.

I have listened with delighted attention to some

of the highest eloquence, the pulpits of America and England of the present day can boast. I have seen tears of conviction and penitence flow freely under the sterner truths of the word of God, but it was left for one at Hido, the most obscure corner of those distant islands, to excite the liveliest emotions ever experienced and leave the deepest impressions of the extent and unsearchable riches of the gospel, which I have ever known.

It seemed, even while I gazed, that the majesty of that Power might be seen rising and erecting to itself a throne, permanent as glorious, in the hearts of these but late utterly benighted and deeply-polluted people. And when I compared them, as they had once been known to me, and as they now appeared, the change seemed the effect of a mandate scarcely less mighty in its power or speedy in its result than that exhibited when it was said, "Let there be light," "and there was light!"

The depth of the impression arose from the irresistible conviction that the Spirit of God was there. It could have been nothing else. With the exception of the inferior chiefs, having charge of the district, and their dependents; of two or three native members of the church; and of the mission family, scarce one of the whole multitude was in other than the native dress, the simple garments of their primitive state.

In this respect and in the attitude of sitting, the assembly was purely pagan. But the breathless silence, the eager attention, the half-suppressed sigh, the tear, the various feelings, sad, peaceful, joyous, discoverable in the faces of many—all spoke the presence of an invisible but omnipotent Power—the Power which alone can melt and renew the heart of man, even as it alone first brought it into existence.

It was, in a word, a heathen congregation laying hold on the hopes of eternity—a heathen congregation, fully sensible of the degradation of their original state, exulting in the first beams of truth and in the no uncertain dawning of the Sun of Righteousness: thirsting after knowledge, even while they sweetly drank of the waters of life; and, under the inspiring influence, by every look, expressing the heartfelt truth—"Beautiful on the mountains are the feet of him that bringeth good tidings; that bringeth good tidings of good, that publisheth SALVATION!"

The simple appearance and yet Christian deportment of that obscure congregation, whom I had once known, and at no remote period, only as a set of rude, licentious, and wild pagans, did more to rivet the conviction of the divine origin of the Bible and of the holy influences by which it is accompanied to the hearts of men, than all the arguments and apologies and defences of Christianity I ever read.

An entire moral reformation has taken place. Instruction of every kind is eagerly and universally sought, and from many an humble dwelling, now

"Is daily heard
The voice of prayer and praise to Jacob's God
And many a heart in secret heaves the sigh,
To Him who hears, well pleased,
　　the sigh contrite."

QUESTIONS — 1. Why was the author qualified to judge the effects of Christianity on this newly-converted group? 2. According to the author, why were the Hawaiian people so grateful for their new knowledge of salvation? 3. What effect did this scene have on the author's appreciation of the Bible?

SPELL AND DEFINE — (1) uninterrupted, procession; (2) multitudes; (3) remembrances, re-echoed, assembling; (4) hundred, irregular, inhabitants; (5) calculated, apprized, conclusion; (6) midshipmen, impracticability; (8) congregation, appendages; (10) majesty, permanent, benighted.

LESSON VI (6)

Speech of Logan—JEFFERSON

NOTE—"Logan was the English name of the Indian Chief Tahgah-jute (c. 1725–1780). . . . The massacre of his family in 1774—with which Cresap probably had no connection—did lead him to instigate the war here described; and Logan did refuse to sue for peace; but the authenticity of the speech itself is doubtful. . . ." The speech was first published in Thomas Jefferson's *Notes on Virginia.* (Stanley W. Lindberg, *The Annotated McGuffey: Selections from the McGuffey Eclectic Readers,* 1836–1920, New York: Van Nostrand Reinhold Com., © 1976, pp. 248, 249. Reprinted by permission of the publisher.)

I may challenge the whole of the orations of Demosthenes and Cicero and, indeed, of any more eminent orators, if Europe or the world has furnished more eminent, to produce a single passage superior to the speech of Logan, a Mingo chief, delivered to Lord Dunmore when he was governor of Virginia. As a testimony of Indian talents in this line, I beg leave to introduce it by first stating the incidents necessary for understanding it.

In the spring of the year 1774, a robbery was committed by some Indians upon certain land adventurers on the Ohio river. The whites in that quarter, according to their custom, undertook to punish this outrage in a summary way. Captain Michael Cresap and one Daniel Greathouse, leading on these parties, surprised at different times, traveling and hunting parties of the Indians, who had their women and children with them, and murdered many. Among these were unfortunately the family of Logan, a chief celebrated in peace and war and long distinguished as the friend of the whites.

This unworthy return provoked his vengeance. He accordingly signalized himself in the war which ensued. In the autumn of the same year a decisive battle was fought at the mouth of the Great Kenhawa, between the collected forces of the Shawnees, the Mingoes, and the Delawares, and a detachment of the Virginia militia. The Indians were defeated and sued for peace. Logan, however, disdained to be seen among the suppliants, but, lest the sincerity of a treaty, from which so distinguished a chief absented himself, should be distrusted, he sent by a messenger the following speech to be delivered to Lord Dunmore.

"I appeal to any white man to say, if ever he entered Logan's cabin hungry, and he gave him not meat; if ever he came cold and naked, and he clothed him not. During the course of the last long and bloody war, Logan remained idle in his cabin, an advocate for peace. Such was my love for the whites that my countrymen pointed as they passed, and said, 'Logan is the friend of the white men.' I had even thought to live with you, but for the injuries of one man. Colonel Cresap, last spring in cold blood and unprovoked, murdered all the relatives of Logan, not sparing even my women and children. There runs not a drop of my blood in the veins of any living creature. This called on me for revenge. I have sought it. I have killed many. I have fully glutted my vengeance. For my country, I rejoice at the beams of peace. But do not harbor a thought that mine is the joy of fear: Logan never felt fear. He will not turn on his heel to save his life. Who is there to mourn for Logan? Not one."

QUESTIONS — 1. The names of Demosthenes and Cicero would have been familiar to advanced students who first read this FOURTH READER. If you do not know anything about them, check their names in an encyclopedia. 2. Why did Chief Logan make this speech?

SPELL AND DEFINE — (1) challenge; (2) outrage, summary; (3) signalized, detachment, glutted, harbor.

LESSON VII (7)

Death of Absalom—BIBLE

NOTE—Absalom, the handsome and popular son of King David, schemed against his father to obtain the kingship and had himself proclaimed king at Hebron. Marching against Jerusalem, he forced David to flee the capital and took possession of the royal palace and of the harem. The following episode relates the events of battle when David's and Absalom's armies finally met.

II Samuel 18

1. And David numbered the people that were with him, and set captains of thousands and captains of hundreds over them.

2. And David sent forth a third part of the people under the hand of Joab, and a third part under the hand of Abishai the son of Zeruiah, Joab's brother, and a third part under the hand of Ittai the Gittite. And the king said unto the people, I will surely go forth with you myself also.

3. But the people answered, Thou shalt not go forth: for if we flee away, they will not care for us; neither if half of us die, will they care for us; but now thou art worth ten thousand of us: therefore now it is better that thou succor us out of the city.

4. And the king said unto them, What seemeth you best I will do. And the king stood by the gate

side, and all the people came out by hundreds and by thousands.

5. And the king commanded Joab and Abishai and Ittai, saying, Deal gently for my sake with the young man, even with Absalom. And all the people heard when the king gave all the captains charge concerning Absalom.

6. So the people went out into the field against Israel; and the battle was in the wood of Ephraim;

7. Where the people of Israel were slain before the servants of David, and there was there a great slaughter that day of twenty thousand men.

8. For the battle was there scattered over the face of all the country: and the wood devoured more people that day than the sword devoured.

9. And Absalom met the servants of David. And Absalom rode upon a mule, and the mule went under the thick boughs of a great oak, and his head caught hold of the oak, and he was taken up between the heaven and the earth and the mule that was under him went away.

10. And a certain man saw it, and told Joab, and said, Behold, I saw Absalom hanged in an oak.

11. And Joab said unto the man that told him, And behold, thou sawest him, and why didst thou not smite him there to the ground? And I would have given thee ten shekels of silver, and a girdle.

12. And the man said unto Joab, Though I should receive a thousand shekels of silver in my hand, yet would I not put forth my hand against the king's son: for in our hearing the king charged thee and Abishai and Ittai, saying, Beware that none touch the young man Absalom.

13. Otherwise I should have wrought falsehood against mine own life: for there is no matter hid

from the king, and thou thyself wouldst have set thyself against me.

14. Then said Joab, I may not tarry thus with thee. And he took three darts in his hand, and thrust them through the heart of Absalom, while he was yet alive in the midst of the oak.

15. And ten young men that bare Joab's armor compassed about and smote Absalom, and slew him.

16. And Joab blew the trumpet, and the people returned from pursuing after Israel; for Joab held back the people.

17. And they took Absalom, and cast him into a great pit in the wood, and laid a very great heap of stones upon him: and all Israel fled every one to his tent.

18. Now Absalom in his lifetime had taken and reared up for himself a pillar, which is in the king's dale; for he said, I have no son to keep my name in remembrance; and he called the pillar after his own name, and it is called unto this day, Absalom's Place.

19. Then said Ahimaaz the son of Zadok, Let me now run, and bear the king tidings, how that the Lord hath avenged him of his enemies.

20. And Joab said unto him, Thou shalt not bear tidings this day, but thou shalt bear tidings another day: but this day thou shalt bear no tidings, because the king's son is dead.

21. Then said Joab to Cushi, Go tell the king what thou hast seen. And Cushi bowed himself unto Joab, and ran.

22. Then said Ahimaaz the son of Zadok yet again to Joab, But howsoever, let me, I pray thee, also run after Cushi. And Joab said, Wherefore wilt

thou run, my son, seeing that thou hast no tidings ready!

23. But howsoever, said he, let me run. And he said unto him, run. Then Ahimaaz ran by the way of the plain, and overran Cushi.

24. And David sat between the two gates: and the watchman went up to the roof over the gate unto the wall, and lifted up his eyes, and looked, and behold a man running alone.

25. And the watchman cried, and told the king. And the king said, If he be alone there is tidings in his mouth. And he came apace, and drew near.

26. And the watchman saw another man running: and the watchman called unto the porter, and said, Behold, another man running alone. And the king said, He also bringeth tidings.

27. And the watchman said, Methinketh the running of the foremost is like the running of Ahimaaz the son of Zadok. And the king said, He is a good man, and cometh with good tidings.

28. And Ahimaaz called, and said unto the king, All is well. And he fell down to the earth upon his face before the king, and said, Blessed be the Lord thy God, which hath delivered up the men that lifted up their hand against my lord the king.

29. And the king said, Is the young man Absalom safe? And Ahimaaz answered, When Joab sent the king's servant and me thy servant, I saw a great tumult, but I knew not what it was.

30. And the king said unto him, Turn aside and stand here. And he turned aside, and stood still.

31. And behold, Cushi came; and Cushi said, Tidings my lord the king; for the Lord hath avenged thee this day of all them that rose up against thee.

32. And the king said unto Cushi, Is the young

man Absalom safe? And Cushi answered, The enemies of my lord the king, and all that rise against
thee to do thee hurt, be as that young man is.

33. And the king was much moved, and went up
to the chamber over the gate, and wept; and as he
went, thus he said, O my son Absalom! my son, my
son Absalom! would God I had died for thee, O
Absalom, my son, my son.

QUESTIONS — 1. Why didn't David himself go forth to the
battle? 2. What charge did David give to the three officers in
regard to Absalom? 3. What motives probably influenced Joab
to such a course of cruelty? 4. What was the effect of the news
of Absalom's death upon King David?

SPELL AND DEFINE — (1) thousands; (3) succor; (5) concerning; (6) Ephraim; (7) slaughter; (11) shekels; (13) otherwise;
(15) compassed; (18) remembrance; (19) Ahimaaz; (25) watchman; (27) methinketh; (29) tumult; (31) avenged.

LESSON VIII (8)

Absalom—WILLIS

NOTE— In this poem the poet tries to express the emotions of
David for this son—during Absalom's rebellion and after his
death.

King David's limbs were weary. He had fled
From far Jerusalem; and now he stood,
With his faint people, for a little rest
Upon the shore of Jordan. The light wind
Of morn was stirring, and he bared his brow
To its refreshing breath; for he had worn
The mourner's cover, and he had not felt
That he could see his people until now.

They gathered round him on the fresh green bank
And spoke their kindly words; and, as the sun
Rose up in heaven, he knelt among them there,
And bowed his head upon his hands to pray.
Oh! when the heart is full—when bitter thoughts
Come crowding thickly up for utterance,
And the poor common words of courtesy
Are such a very mockery—how much
The bursting heart may pour itself in prayer!
He prayed for Israel; and his voice went up
Strongly and fervently. He prayed for those
Whose love had been his shield; and his deep tones
Grew tremulous. But, oh! for Absalom—
For his estranged, misguided Absalom—
The proud, bright being, who had burst away,
In all his princely beauty, to defy
The heart that cherished him—for him he poured,
In agony that would not be controlled,
Strong supplication, and forgave him there,
Before his God for his deep sinfulness.

•   •   •

The pall was settled. He who slept beneath
Was straightened for the grave; and, as the folds
Sunk to the still proportions, they betrayed
The matchless symmetry of Absalom.
His hair was yet unshorn, and silken curls
Were floating round the tassels as they swayed
To the admitted air, as glossy now
As when, in hours of gentle dalliance, bathing
The snowy fingers of Judea's girls.
His helm was at his feet: his banner, soiled
With trailing through Jerusalem, was laid,
Reversed, beside him: and the jeweled hilt,
Whose diamonds lit the passage of his blade,
Rested, like mockery, on his covered brow.
The soldiers of the king trod to and fro,

Clad in the garb of battle; and their chief,
The mighty Joab, stood beside the bier,
And gazed upon the dark pall steadfastly,
As if he feared the slumberer might stir.
A slow step startled him. He grasped his blade
As if a trumpet rang; but the bent form
Of David entered, and he gave command,
In a low tone, to his few followers,
Who left him with his dead. The king stood still
Till the last echo died: then, throwing off
The sackcloth from his brow, and laying back
The pall from the still features of his child,
He bowed his head upon him, and broke forth
In the resistless eloquence of woe:—

"Alas! my noble boy! that thou should'st die!
    Thou, who were made so beautifully fair!
That death should settle in thy glorious eye,
    And leave his stillness in this clustering hair!
How could he mark thee for the silent tomb,
        My proud boy, Absalom!

"Cold is thy brow, my son! and I am chill,
    As to my bosom I have tried to press thee.
How was I wont to feel my pulses thrill,
    Like a rich harp-string, yearning to caress thee,
And hear thy sweet "*my father*" from these dumb
        And cold lips, Absalom!

"The grave hath won thee. I shall hear the gush
    Of music and the voices of the young;
And life will pass me in the mantling blush,
    And the dark tresses to the soft winds flung,
But thou no more, with thy sweet voice, shalt come
        To meet me, Absalom!

"And, oh! when I am stricken, and my heart,
    Like a bruised reed, is waiting to be broken,

How will its love for thee, as I depart,
  Yearn for thine ear to drink its last deep token!
It were so sweet, amid death's gathering gloom,
        To see thee, Absalom!

"And now, farewell! 'Tis hard to give thee up,
  With death so like a gentle slumber on thee:—
And thy dark sin! —Oh! I could drink the cup,
  If from this woe its bitterness had won thee.
May God have called thee, like a wanderer, home,
        My erring Absalom!"

He covered up his face, and bowed himself
A moment on his child: then, giving him
A look of melting tenderness, he clasped
His hand convulsively, as if in prayer;
And, as a strength were given him of God,
He rose up calmly, and composed the pall
Firmly and decently, and left him there,
As if his rest had been a breathing sleep.

QUESTIONS — 1. What facts does the poet alter in order to create a stage for David to pour forth his words of mourning? 2. Point out the careful wording that contrasts Joab beside the bier and David as he approaches his dead son. (3) In David's soliloquy what things does he say he will miss because of Absalom's death? 4. What does the last stanza reveal about David's mourning?

SPELL AND DEFINE — mourners, bitter, courtesy, mockery, misguided, estranged, cherished, controlled, straightened, matchless, symmetry, tassels, reversed, jeweled, hilt, steadfastly, sackcloth, eloquence.

LESSON IX (9)

Charles II and William Penn—WEEMS

NOTE—William Penn was a famous English Quaker who founded Pennsylvania. The influence of the Frame of Governement, which he drew up for his colony, is noticeable even in the Constitution of the United States.

Parson Weems, the author of this dialogue (and the story of George Washington and the hatchet) is here making a hero of Penn by having him stand up to an English king and address him in fearless logic. Such a scene obviously appealed to American audiences. (Lindberg 239, 241.)

King Charles: Well, friend William! I have sold you a noble province in North America, but still, I suppose you have no thought of going there yourself.

Penn: Yes, I have, I assure thee, friend Charles; and I am just come to bid thee farewell.

K.C.: What! venture yourself among the savages of North America! Why, man, what security have you that you will not be in their war kettle in two hours after setting foot on their shores?

P.: The best security in the world.

K.C.: I doubt that, friend William. I have no idea of any security against those cannibals, but in a regiment of good soldiers with their muskets and bayonets. And mind, I tell you beforehand, that, with all my good will for you and your family, to whom I am under obligations, I will not send a single soldier with you.

P.: I want none of thy soldiers, Charles: I depend on something better than thy soldiers.

K.C.: Ah! what may that be?

P.: Why, I depend upon themselves; on the working of their own hearts; on their notions of justice; on their moral sense.

K.C.: A fine thing, this same moral sense, no doubt; but I fear you will not find much of it among the Indians of North America.

P.: And why not among them, as well as others?

K.C.: Because if they had possessed any, they would not have treated my subjects so barbarously as they have done.

P.: That is no proof of the contrary, friend Charles. Thy subjects were the aggressors. When thy subjects first went to North America, they found these poor people the fondest and kindest creatures in the world. Everyday they would watch for them to come ashore and hasten to meet them and feast them on the best fish and venison and corn, which were all they had. In return for this hospitality of the savages, as we call them, thy subjects, termed Christians, seized on their country and rich hunting grounds for farms for themselves. Now, is it to be wondered at, that these much injured people should have been driven to desperation by such injustice and that, burning with revenge, they should have committed some excesses?

K.C.: Well, then, I hope you will not complain when they come to treat you in the same manner.

P.: I am not afraid of it.

K.C.: Ah! how will you avoid it? You mean to get their hunting grounds too, I suppose?

P.: Yes, but not by driving these poor people away from them.

K.C.: No, indeed? How then will you get their lands?

P.: I mean to *buy* their lands from them.

K.C.: *Buy* their lands from *them*? Why, man, you have already bought them of *me*.

P.: Yes, I know I have, and at a dear rate, too, but I did it only to get thy goodwill, not that I thought thou hadst any right to their lands.

K.C.: How, man? No *right* to their lands?

P.: No, friend Charles, no right, no right at all. What right hast thou to their lands?

K.C.: Why, the right of *discovery*, to be sure—the right which the pope and all Christian kings have agreed to give one another.

P.: The right of discovery? A strange kind of right, indeed. Now, suppose, friend Charles, that some canoe load of these Indians, crossing the sea, and discovering this island of Great Britain, were to claim it as their own and set it up for sale over thy head? What wouldst thou think of it?

K.C.: Why—why—why—I must confess, I should think it a piece of great impudence in them.

P.: Well, then, how canst thou, a Christian, and a *Christian prince* too, do that which thou so utterly condemnest in these people, whom thou callest savages? Yes, friend Charles, and suppose again, that these Indians, on thy refusal to give up thy island of Great Britain, were to make war on thee, and having weapons more destructive than thine, were to destroy many of thy subjects and drive the rest away,—wouldst thou not think it horribly cruel?

K.C.: I must say, friend William, that I should. How can I say otherwise?

P.: Well, then, how can I, who call myself a Christian, do what I should abhor even in the heathen? No. I will not do it. But I will buy the right of the proper owners, even of the Indians themselves. By doing this, I shall imitate God himself in His justice and mercy and thereby insure His blessing in my colony, if I should ever live to plant one in North America.

QUESTIONS — 1. How does the author of this dialogue view the American Indians? 2. Upon what was the king's right of ownership based? 3. By what reasoning did Penn convince the king that North America did not belong to him? 4. How did Penn propose to secure the goodwill of the Indians?

SPELL AND DEFINE — savages, security, bayonets, subjects, barbarously, proof, aggressors, desperation, revenge, excesses, discovery, impudence, imitate.

LESSON X (10)

God's First Temples—W. C. BRYANT

NOTE—William Cullen Bryant's father, a country doctor who collected herbs for his own medicines, taught his son botany. When later as a lawyer in Great Barrington, Massachusetts, Bryant hiked through the surrounding countryside, he boasted that he could name "every tree, flower, and spire of grass" in the Berkshires.

1. The groves were God's first temples.
    Ere man learned
  To hew the shaft, and lay the architrave,
  And spread the roof above them—ere he framed
  The lofty vault to gather and roll back
5. The sound of anthems—in the darkling wood,
  Amid the cool and silence, he knelt down
  And offered to the Mightiest solemn thanks
  And supplication. For his simple heart
  Might not resist the sacred influences,
10. That, from the stilly twilight of the place,

And from the gray old trunks,
    that high in heaven
Mingled their mossy boughs,
    and from the sound
Of the invisible breath, that swayed at once
All their green tops, stole over them, and bowed
15. His spirit, with the thought of boundless Power
And inaccessible Majesty. Ah, why
Should we, in the world's riper years, neglect
God's ancient sanctuaries, and adore
Only among the crowd, and under roofs
20. That our frail hands have raised!
       Let me, at least
Here, in the shadow of this aged wood,
Offer one hymn; thrice happy, if it find
Acceptance in His ear.

      Father, thy hand
Hath reared these venerable columns. Thou
25. Didst weave this verdant roof.
     Thou didst look down
Upon the naked earth, and, forthwith, rose
All these fair ranks of trees. They, in thy sun
Budded, and shook their green leaves
    in thy breeze,
And shot toward heaven.
     The century-living crow,
30. Whose birth was in their tops,
    grew old and died
Among their branches; till, at last, they stood,
As now they stand, massy, and tall, and dark,
Fit shrine for humble worshiper to hold
Communion with his Maker. Here are seen
35. No traces of man's pomp, or pride; no silks
Rustle, no jewels shine, nor envious eyes
Encounter; no fantastic carvings show
The boast of our vain race to change the form

Of thy fair works. But thou art here; thou fill'st
40. The solitude. Thou art in the soft winds,
That run along the summits of these trees
In music; thou art in the cooler breath,
That, from the inmost darkness of the place,
Comes, scarcely felt;
      the barky trunks, the ground,
45. The fresh, moist ground,
      are all instinct with thee.
Here is continual worship; nature, here,
In the tranquility that thou dost love,
Enjoys thy presence. Noiselessly, around,
From perch to perch, the solitary bird
50. Passes; and yon clear spring, that,
      'mid its herbs,
Wells softly forth, and visits the strong roots
Of half the mighty forest, tells no tale
Of all the good it does. Thou hast not left
Thyself without a witness, in these shades,
55. Of thy perfections.
      Grandeur, strength, and grace,
Are here to speak of thee. This mighty oak,
By whose immovable stem I stand, and seem
Almost annihilated, not a prince,
In all the proud old world beyond the deep,
60. E'er wore his crown as loftily as he
Wears the green coronal of leaves, with which
Thy hand has graced him. Nestled at his root
Is beauty, such as blooms not in the glare
Of the broad sun. That delicate forest flower,
65. With scented breath, and look so like a smile,
Seems, as it issues from the shapeless mold,
An emanation of the indwelling Life,
A visible token of the upholding Love,
That are the soul of this wide universe.
70. My heart is awed within me, when I think
Of the great miracle that still goes on,

In silence, round me; the perpetual work
Of thy creation, finished, yet renewed
Forever. Written on thy works, I read
75. The lesson of thy own eternity.
Lo! all grow old and die: but see, again,
How on the faltering footsteps of decay
Youth presses, ever gay and beautiful youth,
In all its beautiful forms. These lofty trees
80. Wave not less proudly than their ancestors
Molder beneath them. O, there is not lost
One of earth's charms: upon her bosom yet,
After the flight of untold centuries,
The freshness of her far beginning lies,
85. And yet shall lie. Life mocks the idle hate
Of his arch enemy, Death; yea, seats himself
Upon the sepulcher, and blooms and smiles;
And of the triumphs of his ghastly foe
Makes his own nourishment. For he came forth
90. From thine own bosom, and shall have no end.
There have been holy men, who hid themselves
Deep in the woody wilderness, and gave
Their lives to thought and prayer,
     till they outlived
The generation born with them, nor seemed
95. Less aged than the hoary trees and rocks
Around them; and there have been holy men,
Who deemed it were not well to pass life thus.
But let me often to these solitudes
Retire, and in thy presence, reassure
100. My feeble virtue. Here, its enemies,
The passions, at thy plainer footsteps, shrink,
And tremble, and are still. O God! when thou
Dost scare the world with tempests, set on fire
The heavens with falling thunderbolts, or fill
105. With all the waters of the firmament,
The swift, dark whirlwind,
     that uproots the woods

And drowns the villages; when, at thy call,
Uprises the great deep, and throws himself
Upon the continent, and overwhelms
110. Its cities;—who forgets not, at the sight
Of these tremendous tokens of thy power,
His pride, and lays his strifes and follies by?
O, from these sterner aspects of thy face
Spare me and mine; nor let us need the wrath
115. Of the mad, unchained elements, to teach
Who rules them. Be it ours to meditate,
In these calm shades, thy milder majesty,
And to the beautiful order of thy works,
Learn to conform the order of our lives.

QUESTIONS — 1. What question does Bryant ask in the first section of the poem? 2. What detractions from worship are NOT found in the groves? 3. How does the forest respond to death? 4. The poet says he wants to learn of God in "these calm shades" instead of being taught through what other manifestations of God in nature?

SPELL AND DEFINE — (8) supplication; (13) invisible; (16) inaccessible; (47) tranquility; (60) loftily; (69) universe; (80) ancestors; (87) sepulcher; (98) solitudes; (105) firmament; (116) meditate; (119) conform.

LESSON XI (11)

The Pebble and the Acorn
MISS H. F. GOULD

NOTE—This poem uses the personification of a pebble and an acorn to teach a lesson. Following in the tradition of Judges 9:8-15, the things of nature converse with one another.

"I am a Pebble! and yield to none!"
Were the swelling words of a tiny stone;
"Nor time nor seasons can alter me;
I am abiding, while ages flee.
The pelting hail and the driveling rain
Have tried to soften me, long, in vain;
And the tender dew has sought to melt
Or touch my heart; but it was not felt.

"There's none that can tell about my birth,
For I'm as old as the big, round earth.
The children of men arise, and pass
Out of the world, like blades of grass,
And many a foot on me has trod,
That's gone from sight, and under the sod!
I am a Pebble! but who art *thou*,
Rattling along from the restless bough!"

The Acorn was shocked at this rude salute,
And lay for a moment, abashed and mute;
She never before had been so near
This gravelly ball, the mundane sphere;
And she felt, for a time, at a loss to know
How to answer a thing so coarse and low.

But to give reproof of a nobler sort
Than the angry look, or keen retort,

At length, she said, in a gentle tone:
"Since it has happened that I am thrown
From the lighter element, where I grew,
Down to another, so hard and new,
And beside a personage so august,
Abased, I will cover my head in dust,
And quickly retire from the sight of one
Whom time, nor season, nor storm, nor sun,
Nor the gentle dew, nor the grinding heel,
Has ever subdued, or made to feel!"
And soon, in the earth, she sunk away
From the comfortless spot where the Pebble lay.

But it was not long ere the soil was broke
By the peering head of an infant oak!
And, as it arose, and its branches spread,
The Pebble looked up, and wondering said:
"A *modest Acorn!* never to tell
What was enclosed in its simple shell!
That the pride of the forest was folded up
In the narrow space of its little cup!
And meekly to sink in the darksome earth,
Which proves that nothing could hide its worth!

"And oh! how many will tread on me,
To come and admire the beautiful tree,
Whose head is towering toward the sky,
Above such a worthless thing as I!
Useless and vain, a cumberer here,
I have been idling from year to year.
But never, from this, shall a vaunting word
From the humble Pebble again be heard,
Till something, without me or within,
Shall show the purpose for which I have been."
The Pebble its vow could not forget,
And it lies there wrapped in silence yet.

QUESTIONS — 1. What was the Pebble's boast? 2. How did the Acorn react to the Pebble's rude welcome? 3. How did the Pebble's attitude change? 4. What is the moral of this story-poem?

SPELL AND DEFINE — (1) pelting, driveling; (2) sod; (3) sphere; (4) personage, august, subdued; (6) towering.

LESSON XII (12)

The Necessity of Education
LYMAN BEECHER

NOTE—Throughout his READERS McGuffey declared education to be essential for understanding God's will and for usefulness in this world.

In this essay *East* means that part of the United States east of the Alleghenies; *West* means all of the states and territories west of that mountain range.

The author of this selection, Lyman Beecher, was one of the most popular and influential clergymen of his time. Henry Ward Beecher and Harriet Beecher Stowe were two of his 13 children.

We must educate! We must educate! or we must perish by our own prosperity. If we do not, short will be our race from the cradle to the grave. If, in our haste to be rich and mighty, we outrun our literary and religious institutions, they will never overtake us; or only come up after the battle of liberty is fought and lost, as spoils to grace the victory and as resources of inexorable despotism for the perpetuity of our bondage.

But what will become of the West if her prosperity rushes up to such a majesty of power, while those great institutions linger which are necessary to form the mind and the conscience and the heart of that vast world? It must not be permitted. And yet what is done must be done quickly, for population will not wait, and commerce will not cast anchor, and manufacturers will not shut off the steam nor shut down the gate, and agriculture, pushed by millions of freemen on their fertile soil, will not withhold her corrupting abundance.

And let no man at the East quiet himself and dream of liberty, whatever may become of the West. Our alliance of blood and political institutions and common interests is such that we can not stand aloof in the hour of her calamity, should it ever come. *Her* destiny is *our* destiny. And the day that her gallant ship goes down, our little boat sinks in the vortex!

The great experiment is now making, and from its extent and rapid filling up, is determining in the West, whether the perpetuity of our republican institutions can be reconciled with universal suffrage. Without the education of the *head* and *heart* of the nation, they can not be; and the question to be decided is, can the nation, or the vast balance power of it, be so imbued with intelligence and virtue as to bring out, in laws and their administration, a perpetual self-preserving energy? We know that the work is a vast one and of great difficulty; and yet we believe it can be done.

I am aware that our ablest patriots are looking out on the deep, vexed with storms, with great forebodings and failings of heart for fear of the things that are coming upon us; and I perceive a spirit of impatience rising, and distrust in respect to the perpetuity of our republic; and I am sure that these fears are well founded and am glad that they exist. It is the star of hope in our dark horizon. Fear is what we need, as the ship needs wind on a rocking sea, after a storm, to prevent foundering. But when our fear and our efforts shall correspond with our danger, the danger is past.

For it is not the impossibility of self-preservation which threatens us; nor is it the unwillingness of the nation to pay the price of the *preservation*, as she has paid the price of the *purchase* of our liberties. It is *inattention* and *inconsideration*, protracted till the crisis is past, and the things which belong to our peace are hid from our eyes. And blessed be God, that the tokens of a national waking up, the harbinger of God's mercy, are multiplying upon us!

We did not in the darkest hour believe that God had brought our fathers to this goodly land to lay the foundation of religious liberty, and wrought such wonders in their preservation, and raised their descendants to such heights of civil and religious liberty, only to reverse the analogy of His providence and abandon His work.

And though there now be clouds and the sea roaring and men's hearts failing, we believe there is light behind the cloud, and that the imminence of our danger is intended, under the guidance of Heaven, to call forth and apply a holy, fraternal fellowship between the East and the West, which shall secure our preservation and make the prosperity of our nation durable as time and as abundant as the waves of the sea.

I would add, as a motive to immediate action, that, if we do fail in our great experiment of self-government, our destruction will be as signal as the birthright abandoned, the mercies abused, and the provocation offered to beneficent Heaven. The descent of desolation will correspond with the past elevation.

No punishments of Heaven are so severe as those for mercies abused; and no instrumentality employed in their infliction is so dreadful as the wrath of man. No spasms are like the spasms of expiring liberty, and no wailing such as her convulsions extort.

It took Rome three hundred years to die; and our death, if we perish, will be as much more terrific, as our intelligence and free institutions have given us more bone, sinew, and vitality. May God hide from me the day when the dying agonies of my country shall begin! O, thou beloved land, bound together by the ties of brotherhood and common interest and perils, live forever—one and undivided!

QUESTIONS — 1. Why is *abundance* corrupting? 2. This essay appeared in the first edition (1837) of the FOURTH READER. What might have been causing Beecher's forebodings for the "perpetuity of our republic"? 3. What divisions among people or geographical sections does this country suffer today? 4. What can be the advantage of a spirit of fear? 5. In the original edition McGuffey asked the question: Can the nation continue free without the influence of education and religion? How would you answer his question today?

LESSON XIII (13)

The Scriptures and the Savior
ROUSSEAU

NOTE—Socrates was a Greek philosopher who lived more than 400 years before the birth of Christ. Because of his teachings, influential Athenians eventually brought him to trial for corrupting the young and showing disrespect for religious tradition. He was found guilty and sentenced to death, which he carried out by calmly drinking a cup of hemlock poison. Writers have often compared and contrasted Socrates and Jesus Christ.

The majesty of the Scriptures strikes me with astonishment, and the sanctity of the gospel addresses itself to my heart. Look at the volumes of the philosophers, with all their pomp: how contemptible do they appear in comparison with this! Is it possible that a book at once so simple and sublime can be the work of man!

Can he who is the subject of its history, be himself a mere man? Was his the tone of an enthusiast, or of an ambitious sectary? What sweetness! What purity in his manners! What an affecting gracefulness in his instructions! What sublimity in his maxims! What profound wisdom in his discourses! What presence of mind, what sagacity and propriety in his answers! How great the command over his passions! Where is the man, where the philosopher, who could so live, suffer, and die without weakness and without ostentation!

When Plato described his imaginary good man, covered with all the disgrace of crime, yet worthy of all the rewards of virtue, he described exactly the character of Jesus Christ. The resemblance was so striking, it could not be mistaken, and all the fathers of the church perceived it. What prepossession, what blindness must it be, to compare the son of Sophronius to the son of Mary! What an immeasurable distance between them! Socrates, dying without pain and without ignominy, easily supported his character to the last; and if his death, however easy, had not crowned his life, it might have been doubted whether Socrates, with all his wisdom, was anything more than a mere sophist.

He invented, it is said, the theory of moral science. Others, however, had before him put it in practice; and he had nothing to do but to tell what they had done and to reduce their examples to precept. Aristides had been just, before Socrates defined what justice was. Leonidas had died for his country, before Socrates made it a duty to love one's country. Sparta had been temperate, before Socrates eulogized sobriety; and before he celebrated the praises of virtue, Greece had abounded in virtuous men.

But from whom of all his countrymen could Jesus have derived that sublime and pure morality of which he only has given us both the precepts and example? In the midst of the most licentious fanaticism, the voice of the sublimest wisdom was heard; and the simplicity of the most heroic virtue crowned one of the humblest of all the multitude.

The death of Socrates, peaceably philosophizing with his friends, is the most pleasant that could be desired! That of Jesus, expiring in torments, outraged, reviled, and denounced by a whole nation, is the most horrible that could be feared. Socrates, in receiving the cup of poison, blessed the weeping executioner who presented it; but Jesus, in the midst of excruciating torture, prayed for his merciless tormentors.

Yes! if the life and death of Socrates were those of

a sage, the life and death of Jesus were those of a
God. Shall we say that the evangelical history is a
mere fiction? It does not bear the stamp of fiction,
but the contrary. The history of Socrates, which
nobody doubts, is not as well attested as that of
Jesus Christ. Such an assertion in fact only shifts
the difficulty without removing it. It is more inconceivable that a number of persons should have
agreed to fabricate this book, than that one only
should have furnished the subject of it.

The Jewish authors were incapable of the diction,
and strangers to the morality, contained in the
gospel, the marks of whose truth are so striking, so
perfectly inimitable, that the inventor would be a
more astonishing man than the hero.

QUESTIONS — 1. According to the author, how did the source
of Socrates' teachings differ from the source of Jesus' teachings? 2. Compare and contrast the deaths of Socrates and
Jesus. 3. Why is it inconceivable that the Scriptures are fiction?

SPELL AND DEFINE — (1) majesty, philosophers, contemptible; (2) sectary, maxims, ostentation; (3) sophist; (4) eulogize;
(5) licentious; (7) sage, fabricate; (8) inimitable.

LESSON XIV (14)

The Deluge—BIBLE

NOTE—Stories about a flood which destroyed the world have been found among peoples on every continent and even on islands of the Pacific. This worldwide distribution of the flood stories cannot be accidental and must be accepted as evidence for the historicity of the Biblical flood.

Genesis 7

1. And the Lord said unto Noah, Come thou, and all thy house into the ark: for thee have I seen righteous before me in this generation. 2. Of every clean beast thou shalt take to thee by sevens, the male and his female: and of beasts that are not clean by two, the male and his female. 3. Of fowls also of the air by sevens, the male and the female; to keep seed alive upon the face of all the earth. 4. For yet seven days, and I will cause it to rain upon the earth forty days and forty nights: and every living substance that I have made, will I destroy from off the face of the earth.

5. And Noah did according unto all that the Lord commanded him. 6. And Noah was six hundred years old, when the flood of waters was upon the earth.

7. And Noah went in and his sons, and his wife, and his sons' wives with him, into the ark, because of the waters of the flood. 8. Of clean beasts and of beasts that are not clean, and of fowls, and of every thing that creepeth upon the earth there went in 9. two and two unto Noah into the ark, the male and the female, as God had commanded Noah. 10. And it came to pass after seven days, that the waters of the flood were upon the earth.

11. In the sixth hundredth year of Noah's life, in the second month, the seventeenth day of the month, the same day, were all the fountains of the great deep broken up, and the windows of heaven were opened. 12. And the rain was upon the earth forty days and forty nights.

13. In the self same day entered Noah, and Shem, and Ham, and Japheth, the sons of Noah; and Noah's wife, and the three wives of his sons with them, into the ark: 14. They, and every beast after his kind, and all the cattle after their kind, and every creeping thing that creepeth upon the earth after his kind, and every fowl after his kind, every bird of every sort.

15. And they went in unto Noah into the ark, two and two of all flesh, wherein is the breath of life. 16. And they that went in, went in male and female, of all flesh, as God had commanded him. And the Lord shut him in.

17. And the flood was forty days upon the earth; and the waters increased, and bare up the ark, and it was lifted up above the earth. 18. And the waters prevailed, and were increased greatly upon the earth: and the ark went upon the face of the waters. 19. And the waters prevailed exceedingly upon the earth. And all the high hills that were under the whole heavens were covered.

20. Fifteen cubits upward did the waters prevail; and the mountains were covered. 21. And all flesh died that moved upon the earth, both of fowl, and of cattle, and of beast, and of every creeping thing that creepeth upon the earth, and every man. 22. All in whose nostrils was the breath of life, of all that was in the dry land, died.

23. And every living substance was destroyed which was upon the face of the ground, both man, and cattle, and the creeping things, and the fowl of

the heaven; And they were destroyed from the
earth; and Noah only remained alive, and they that
were with him in the ark. 24. And the waters prevailed upon the earth an hundred and fifty days.

QUESTIONS — 1. Why did God destroy the earth by flood?
(See Genesis 6) 2. How extensive was the flood? 3. Who survived the flood? 4. What evidence is there today in nature for a
worldwide flood?

SPELL AND DEFINE — (1) righteous; (4) substance; (18) prevailed; (19) exceedingly; (20) cubits; (22) nostrils.

LESSON XV (15)

Niagara Falls—HOWISON

NOTE—Before the invention of photography, moving pictures,
or television, the McGuffey READERS' detailed descriptions
of animals and natural wonders were an important source of information to students.

The form of the Niagara Falls is that of an irregular semicircle about three quarters of a mile in extent. This is divided into two distinct cascades by
the intervention of Goat Island, the extremity of
which is perpendicular, and in a line with the precipice, over which the water is projected. The cataract
on the Canada side of the river, is called the Horseshoe Falls, from its peculiar form; and that next to
the United States, the American Falls.

The Table Rock, from which the Falls of the Niagara may be contemplated in all their grandeur, lies
on an exact level with the edge of the cataract on
the Canada side and forms a part of the precipice,
over which the water rushes. It derives its name

from the circumstance of its projecting beyond the
cliffs that support it, like the leaf of a table. To gain
this position, it is necessary to descend a steep bank
and to follow a path that winds among shrubbery
and trees, which entirely conceal from the eye the
scene that awaits him who traverses it.

When near the termination of this road, a few
steps carried me beyond all these obstructions, and
a magnificent amphitheater of cataracts burst upon
my view with appalling suddenness and majesty.
However, in a moment the scene was concealed
from my eyes by a dense cloud of spray, which in-
volved me so completely that I did not dare to extri-
cate myself.

A mingled and thunder-like rushing filled my
ears. I could see nothing, except when the wind
made a chasm in the spray, and then tremendous
cataracts seemed to encompass me on every side;
while below, a raging and foaming gulf of undiscov-
erable extent lashed the rocks with its hissing
waves and swallowed, under a horrible obscurity,
the smoking floods that were precipitated into its
bosom.

At first the sky was obscured by clouds, but after
a few minutes the sun burst forth, and the breeze,
subsiding at the same time, permitted the spray to
ascend perpendicularly. A host of pyramidal clouds
rose majestically, one after another, from the abyss
at the bottom of the Falls; and each, when it had
ascended a little above the edge of the cataract, displayed a beautiful rainbow, which, in a few moments, was gradually transferred into the bosom of
the cloud that immediately succeeded.

The spray of the Horseshoe Falls had extended itself through a wide space directly over me, and, receiving the full influence of the sun, exhibited a luminous and magnificent rainbow, which continued

to overarch and irradiate the spot on which I stood, while I enthusiastically contemplated the indescribable scene.

Any person who has nerve enough may plunge his hand into the water of the Horseshoe Falls, after it is projected over the precipice, merely by lying down flat, with his face beyond the edge of the Table Rock, and stretching out his arm to its utmost extent. The experiment is truly a horrible one, and such as I would not wish to repeat; for, even to this day, I feel a shuddering and recoiling sensation when I recollect having been in the posture above described.

The body of water which composes the middle part of the Horseshoe Falls is so immense that it descends nearly two thirds of the space without being ruffled or broken; and the solemn calmness, with which it rolls over the edge of the precipice, is finely contrasted with the perturbed appearance it assumes after having reached the gulf below. But the water, toward each side of the Falls, is shattered the moment it drops over the rock, and loses as it descends, in a great measure, the character of a fluid, being divided into pyramidal-shaped fragments, the bases of which are turned upward.

The surface of the gulf below the cataract presents a very singular aspect, seeming, as it were, filled with an immense quantity of hoar frost, which is agitated by small and rapid undulation. The particles of water are dazzlingly white and do not apparently unite together, as might be supposed, but seem to continue for a time in a state of distinct comminution, and to repel each other with a thrilling and shivering motion, which cannot easily be described.

The road to the bottom of the Falls presents many more difficulties than that which leads to the

Table Rock. After leaving the Table Rock the traveler must proceed down the river nearly half a mile, where he will come to a small chasm in the bank, in which there is a spiral staircase inclosed in a wooden building. By descending the stair, which is seventy or eighty feet in perpendicular height, he will find himself under the precipice, on the top of which he formerly walked. A high but sloping bank extends from its base to the edge of the river; and, on the summit of this, there is a narrow slippery path, covered with angular fragments of rock which leads to the Horseshoe Falls.

The impending cliffs, hung with a profusion of trees and brushwood, overarch this rock and seem to vibrate with the thunders of the cataract. In some places they rise abruptly to the height of one hundred feet and display upon their surfaces fossil shells and the organic remains of a former world, thus sublimely leading the mind to contemplate the convulsions which nature has undergone since the creation.

As the traveler advances, he is frightfully stunned by the appalling noise; clouds of spray sometimes envelop him, and suddenly check his faltering steps; rattlesnakes start from the cavities of the rocks; and the scream of eagles, soaring among the whirlwinds of eddying vapor, which obscure the gulf of the cataract, at intervals announce that the raging waters have hurled some bewildered animal over the precipice. After scrambling among piles of huge rocks that obscure his way, the traveler gains the bottom of the Falls, where the soul can be susceptible only of one emotion, that of uncontrollable terror.

It was not until I had, by frequent excursions to the Falls, in some measure familiarized my mind with their sublimities, that I ventured to explore the recesses of the Great Cataract. The precipice over which it rolls, is very much arched underneath, while the impetus which the water receives in its descent projects it far beyond the cliff, and thus an immense Gothic arch is formed by the rock and the torrent. Twice I entered this cavern, and twice I was obliged to retrace my steps, lest I should be suffocated by the blast of the dense spray that whirled around me. However, the third time I succeeded in advancing about twenty-five yards.

Here darkness began to encircle me. On one side the black cliff stretched itself into a gigantic arch far above my head, and on the other, the dense and hissing torrent formed an impenetrable sheet of foam with which I was drenched in a moment. The rocks were so slippery that I could hardly keep my feet, or hold securely by them, while the horrid din made me think the precipices above were tumbling down in colossal fragments upon my head.

A little way below Horseshoe Falls, the river is, comparatively speaking, so tranquil that a ferry boat plies between the Canadian and American shores for the convenience of travelers. When I first crossed, the heaving flood tossed about the skiff with a violence that seemed very alarming, but as soon as we gained the middle of the river, my attention was altogether engaged by the surpassing grandeur of the scene before me.

I was now in the area of a semicircle of cataracts, more than three thousand feet in extent, and floated on the surface of a gulf—raging, fathomless, and interminable. Majestic cliffs, splendid rainbows, lofty trees, and columns of spray were the gorgeous decorations of this theater of wonders, while a dazzling sun shed refulgent glories upon every part of the scene.

Surrounded with clouds of vapor and stunned

into a state of confusion and terror by the hideous noise, I looked upward to the height of one hundred and fifty feet, and saw vast floods, dense, awful, and stupendous, vehemently bursting over the precipice, and rolling down as if the windows of heaven were opened to pour another deluge upon the earth.

Loud sounds resembling discharges of artillery or volcanic explosions were now distinguishable amid the watery tumult, and added terrors to the abyss from which they issued. The sun, looking majestically through the ascending spray, was encircled by a radiant halo, while fragments of rainbows floated on every side and momentarily vanished, only to give place to a succession of others more brilliant.

Looking backward, I saw the Niagara River, again becoming calm and tranquil, rolling magnificently between the towering cliffs that rose on either side. A gentle breeze ruffled the waters and beautiful birds fluttered around, as if to welcome its egress from those clouds and thunders and rainbows, which were the heralds of its precipitation into the abyss of the cataract.

QUESTIONS — 1. What emotions did the author experience during his encounters with Niagara Falls? 2. Name the beauties and the terrors of Niagara Falls. 3. If you have seen Niagara Falls, contrast your experience with the author's experience.

SPELL AND DEFINE — (2) contemplate, precipice; (3) appalling; (5) majestically; (10) fragments; (12) cavities; (14) gigantic; (15) surpassing, grandeur; (16) fathomless, interminable; (17) stupendous.

LESSON XVI (16)

Contrasted Soliloquies—JANE TAYLOR

NOTE—In the READERS, the lessons that deal with the wonders and mysteries of nature are most often used to establish belief in a God who is both Creator and Sustainer. However, in this selection a different point is being made—and uncharacteristically the moral is not stated at the end. The reader must draw his own conclusion.

"Alas!" exclaimed a silver-headed sage, "how narrow is the utmost extent of human science! How circumscribed the sphere of intellectual exertion! I have spent my life in acquiring knowledge, but how little do I know! The farther I attempt to penetrate the secrets of nature, the more I am bewildered and benighted. Beyond a certain limit, all is but confusion or conjecture, so that the advantage of the learned over the ignorant consists greatly in having ascertained how little is to be known.

"It is true that I can measure the sun and compute the distances of the planets; I can calculate their periodical movements and even ascertain the laws by which they perform their sublime revolutions; but with regard to their construction and the beings which inhabit them, what do I know more than the clown!

"Delighting to examine the economy of nature in our own world, I have analyzed the elements and have given names to their component parts. And yet, should I not be as much at a loss to explain the burning of fire or to account for the liquid quality of water, as the unschooled, who use and enjoy them without thought or examination?

"I remark that all bodies, unsupported, fall to the

ground; and I am taught to account for this by the law of gravitation. But what have I gained here more than a term? Does it convey to my mind any idea of the nature of that mysterious and invisible chain which draws all things to a common center? I observe the effect, I give a name to the cause; but can I explain or comprehend it?

"Pursuing the track of the naturalist, I have learned to distinguish the *animal, vegetable* and *mineral* kingdoms, and to divide these into their distinct tribes and families; but can I tell, after all this toil, whence a single blade of grass derives its vitality? Could the most minute researches enable me to discover the exquisite pencil that paints and fringes the flower of the field? Have I ever detected the secret that gives its brilliant dye to the ruby and the emerald, or the art that enamels the delicate shell?

"I observe the sagacity of animals; I call it *instinct*, and speculate upon its various degrees of approximation to the reason of man. But, after all, I know as little of the cogitations of the brute, as he does of mine. When I see a flight of birds overhead performing their evolutions or steering their course to some distant settlement, their signals and cries are as unintelligible to me as are the learned languages to the unlettered rustic; I understand as little of their policy and laws, as they do of Blackstone's Commentaries.

"But leaving the material creation, my thoughts have often ascended to loftier subjects and indulged in *metaphysical* speculation. And here, while I easily perceive in myself the two distinct qualities of matter and mind, I am baffled in every attempt to comprehend their mutual dependence and mysterious connection. When my hand moves in obedience to my will, have I the most distant conception of the manner in which the volition is either communicated or understood? Thus, in the exercise of one of the most simple and ordinary actions, I am perplexed and confounded if I attempt to account for it.

"Again, how many years of my life were devoted to the acquisition of those *languages*, by the means of which I might explore the records of remote ages and become familiar with the learning and literature of other times! And what have I gathered from these, but the mortifying fact that man has ever been struggling with his own impotence and vainly endeavoring to overleap the bounds which limit his anxious inquiries?

"Alas! then, what have I gained by my laborious researches, but an humbling conviction of my weakness and ignorance? How little has man, at his best estate, of which to boast! What folly in him to glory in his contracted power or to value himself upon his imperfect acquisitions!"

• • •

"Well," exclaimed a young lady, just returned from school, "my education is at last finished! Indeed, it would be strange if, after five years' hard application, any thing were left incomplete. Happily, *that* is all over now, and I have nothing to do but to exercise my various accomplishments.

"Let me see! As to *French*, I am complete mistress of that and speak it, if possible, with more fluency than English. *Italian* I can read with ease and pronounce very well, as well, at least, as any of my friends, and that is all one need wish for in Italian. *Music* I have learned till I am perfectly sick of it. But, now that we have a grand piano, it will be delightful to play when we have company; I must still continue to practice a little—the only thing, I think, that I need now to improve myself in. And then there are my Italian songs which everybody allows I sing with taste, and as it is what so few people can pretend to, I am particularly glad that I can.

"My *drawings* are universally admired—especially the shells and flowers, which are beautiful, certainly. Besides this, I have a decided taste in all kinds of fancy ornaments. And then my *dancing* and *waltzing*, in which our master himself owned that he could take me no farther—just the figure for it, certainly; it would be unpardonable if I did not excel.

"As to *common* things, *geography* and *history* and *poetry* and *philosophy*—thank my stars, I have got through them all, so that I may consider myself not only perfectly accomplished, but also thoroughly well informed. Well, to be sure, how much I have dragged through—the only wonder is, that one head can contain it all!"

QUESTIONS — 1. Define: soliloquy. 2. Who are the two speakers? 3. What is the attitude of each concerning their accomplishments? 4. What lesson does the author want you to learn from these "contrasted soliloquies"?

SPELL AND DEFINE — (1) circumscribed, intellectual, penetrate, conjecture, ascertain; (2) compute, revolutions; (3) economy, component; (4) gravitation; (5) exquisite, vitality; (6) sagacity, instinct, approximation, cogitation; (7) metaphysical, volition; (11) fluency.

LESSON XVII (17)

The Alhambra by Moonlight—IRVING

NOTE—In 1826 Washington Irving, the first American-born author to gain a literary reputation in Europe, went to Spain where he spent seven years. While working on his book *The Alhambra*, he lived for four months in the palace of the Alhambra, where he absorbed a sense of the Spanish soul.

I have given a picture of my apartment on my first taking possession of it. A few evenings have produced a thorough change in the scene and in my feelings. The moon, which then was invisible, has gradually gained upon the nights and now rolls in full splendor above the towers, pouring a flood of tempered light into every court and hall. The garden beneath my window is gently lighted up; the orange and citron trees are tipped with silver; the fountain sparkles in the moonbeams; and even the blush of the rose is faintly visible.

I have sat for hours at my window, inhaling the sweetness of the garden, and musing on the checkered features of those whose history is dimly shadowed out in the elegant memorials around. Sometimes I have issued forth at midnight when everything was quiet and have wandered over the whole building. Who can do justice to a moonlight night in such a climate and in such a place! The temperature of an Andalusian midnight in summer is perfectly ethereal. We seem lifted up into a purer atmosphere; there is a serenity of soul, a buoyancy of spirits, an elasticity of frame, that render mere *existence* enjoyment. The effect of moonlight, too, on the Alhambra, has something like enchantment. Every rent and chasm of time, every mouldering tint and

weather stain, disappears; the marble resumes its
original whiteness; the long colonnades brighten in
the moonbeams; the halls are illuminated with a
softened radiance, until the whole edifice reminds
one of the enchanted palace of an Arabian tale.

At such a time, I have ascended to the little
pavilion, called the queen's toilette, to enjoy its
varied and extensive prospect. To the right, the
snowy summits of the Sierra Nevada, would gleam,
like silver clouds, against the darker firmament,
and all the outlines of the mountain would be softened, yet delicately defined. My delight, however,
would be to lean over the parapet of the Tocador
and gaze down upon Granada, spread out like a map
below me, all buried in deep repose, and its white
palaces and convents sleeping, as it were, in the
moonshine.

Sometimes I would hear the faint sounds of castanets from some party of dancers lingering in the
Alameda; at other times I have heard the dubious
tones of a guitar and the notes of a single voice
rising from some solitary street, and have pictured
to myself some youthful cavalier, serenading his
lady's window, a gallant custom of former days, but
not sadly on the decline, except in the remote towns
and villages of Spain.

Such are the scenes that have detained me for
many an hour, loitering about the courts and bal-
conies of the castle, enjoying that mixture of reverie
and sensation which steal away existence in a
southern climate—and it has been almost morning
before I have retired to my bed and been lulled to
sleep by the falling waters of the fountain of Lin-
daraxa.

QUESTIONS — 1. Why might a palace in Spain have a great effect on one who was American-born? 2. How did the moonlight

change the appearance of the Alhambra? 3. The Alhambra is considered the finest example of Moorish art in Europe. See if you can find a picture of it in an encyclopedia or other reference book.

SPELL AND DEFINE — (1) apartment, splendor; (2) inhaling, memorials, enchantment, colonnades, buoyancy; (3) pavilion, repose, convents; (4) castanets, cavalier, serenading; (5) reverie.

LESSON XVIII (18)

The Elevated Character of Women
CARTER

NOTE—This essay reflects the attitude of society toward women during the nineteenth century. In contrast to much of today's writing on women, it values highly their homemaking and nurturing skills.

The influence of the female character is now felt and acknowledged in all the relations of life. I speak not now of those distinguished women, who instruct their age through the public press. Nor of those whose devout strains we take upon our lips when we worship. But of a much larger class—of those whose influence is felt in the relations of neighbor, friend, daughter, wife, mother.

Who waits at the couch of the sick to administer tender charities while life lingers or to perform the last acts of kindness when death comes? Where shall we look for those examples of friendship that most adorn our nature, those abiding friendships, which trust even when betrayed, and survive all changes of fortune?

Where shall we find the brightest illustrations of filial piety? Have you even seen a daughter watching the decline of an aged parent and holding out with heroic fortitude to anticipate his wishes, to administer to his wants, and to sustain his tottering steps to the very borders of the grave?

But in no relation does woman exercise so deep an influence, both immediately and prospectively, as in that of mother. To her is committed the immortal treasure of the infant mind. Upon her devolves the care of the first stages of that course of discipline which is to form of a being, perhaps the most frail and helpless in the world, the fearless ruler of animated creation, and the devout adorer of its great Creator.

Her smiles call into exercise the first affections that spring up in our hearts. She cherishes and expands the earliest germs of our intellects. She breathes over us her deepest devotions. She lifts our little hands and teaches our little tongues to lisp in prayer.

She watches over us like a guardian angel and protects us through all our helpless years, when we know not of her cares and her anxieties on our account. She follows us into the world of men, and lives in us, and blesses us, when she lives not otherwise upon the earth.

What constitutes the center of every home? Whither do our thoughts turn, when our feet are weary with wandering and our hearts sick with disappointments? Where shall the truant and forgetful husband go for sympathy unalloyed and without design, but to the bosom of her who is ever ready and waiting to share in his adversity or his prosperity? And if there be a tribunal where the sins and the follies of a froward child may hope for pardon and forgiveness this side of heaven, that tribunal is the heart of a fond and devoted mother.

Finally, her influence is felt deeply in religion. "If

Christianity should be compelled to flee from the mansions of the great, the academies of philosophers, the halls of legislators, or the throng of busy men, we should find her last and purest retreat with woman at the fireside; her last altar would be the female heart; her last audience would be the children gathered round the knees of the mother; her last sacrifice, the secret prayer escaping in silence from her lips, and heard, perhaps, only at the throne of God.

QUESTIONS — 1. What does the writer admire about women? 2. Do all women fit the description given here? 3. Which of the praiseworthy characteristics listed here are limited to women only? 4. Which are also characteristics to be praised in men?

SPELL AND DEFINE — (1) distinguished, neighbor, daughter; (2) administer, betrayed; (3) illustrations; (4) exercise, immediately, prospectively; (6) guardian; (7) truant, disappointments, froward; (8) philosophers, legislators.

LESSON XIX (19)

Thirsting After Righteousness—BIBLE

NOTE—When David wrote this psalm, he was a hunted fugitive, living in the caves of the wilderness. He laments his exile from the house of God, where he had found joy in participating in the holy services.

Psalm 42

As the hart panteth after the water brooks,
So panteth my soul after thee, O God!
My soul thirsteth for God, for the living God:
When shall I come and appear before God?
My tears have been my meat day and night,

While they continually say unto me,
    Where is thy God?

When I remember these things,
    I pour out my soul in me:
For I had gone with the multitude,
    I went with them to the house of God,
With the voice of joy and praise,
With a multitude that kept holy-day.

    Why art thou cast down, O my soul?
And why art thou disquieted within me?
Hope thou in God: —for I shall yet praise him
For the help of his countenance.

    O my God! my soul is cast down within me:
Therefore will I remember thee from the land of
    Jordan, and of the Hermonites,
From the hill Mizar.
Deep calleth unto deep,
    at the noise of thy water-spouts;
All thy waves and thy billows are gone over me!
Yet the Lord will command his living kindness
    in the day time,
And in the night his song shall be with me,
And my prayer unto the God of my life.

    I will say unto God my rock,
    Why hast thou forgotten me?
Why go I mourning, because of the
    oppression of the enemy?
As with a sword in my bones,
    mine enemies reproach me;
While they say daily unto me, Where is thy God?

    Why art thou cast down, O my soul?
And why art thou disquieted within me?

Hope thou in God: —for I will yet praise him,
Who is the health of my countenance,
  and my God.

QUESTIONS — 1. The form of this psalm consists of two sections of similar length, each followed by a refrain. Locate the refrains and point out their similarities and differences. 2. What does David remember about going to the house of God? 3. If he cannot worship God in His house, where does David say he will worship Him?

SPELL AND DEFINE — (1) hart; (2) multitude; (3) disquieted, countenance; (4) billows; (5) oppression.

LESSON XX (20)

Writing in Ancient Times
MONTGOMERY

NOTE—The Sumerians are credited with inventing the first system of writing because the earliest documents ever discovered are cuneiform tablets from Sumeria dated around 3000 B.C. In this essay the writer uses internal evidence from the Bible to establish that writing was known in ancient times.

That the art of writing was practiced in Egypt before the emancipation of the Israelites, appears almost certain from their frequent and familiar mention of this method of keeping memorials. When the people had provoked the Lord to wrath by making and worshiping the golden calf, Moses, interceding in their behalf, says, "Yet now, if thou wilt forgive their sin; and if not, blot me, I pray thee, out of thy book which thou hast written. And the Lord said unto Moses, Whosoever sinneth, him will I blot out of my book."

The allusion here is to a table of genealogy, the muster-roll of an army, a register of citizenship, or even to those books of chronicles which were kept by order of ancient oriental princes, of the events of their reigns for reference and remembrance.

Besides, such a method of publishing important documents is alluded to, not merely as nothing new, but as if even the common people were practically acquainted with it. "And thou shalt bind them (the statutes and testimonies of the Lord) as a sign upon thine hand, and they shall be as frontlets between thine eyes, and thou shalt write them upon the posts of thine house, and upon all thy gates." There are various parallel passages which no caviling of commentators can convert from plain meaning into paradox.

But not the Egyptians and Hebrews alone possessed this invaluable knowledge at the time of which we speak (from fourteen to seventeen hundred years before Christ). We have direct and incidental testimony, both in sacred and secular history, that the Phoenicians, Arabians, and Chaldeans were instructed in the same. The book of Job lays the scene and the season of his affliction about this era, and in the north of Arabia.

That extraordinary composition—extraordinary indeed, whether it be regarded as an historical, dramatic, or poetic performance—contains more curious and minute information concerning the manners and customs, the literature and philosophy, the state of arts and sciences, during the patriarchal ages, than can be collected in scattered hints from all later works put together.

In reference to the art and the materials of writing then in use, we meet with the following sublime and affecting apostrophe— "O that my words were now written! O that they were printed

(impressed or traced out) in a book! That they were
graven with an iron pen and lead, in the rock for
ever!"

The latter aspiration probably alludes to the very
ancient practice of hewing characters into the faces
of vast rocks as eternal memorials of persons and
events. It is said by travelers whose testimony
seems worthy of credence, that various fragments
of such inscriptions, now utterly undecipherable,
may be seen to this day in the wilderness of Arabia
Petrea—monuments at once of the grasp and the
limitation of the mental power of man; thus making
the hardest substances in nature the depositories of
his thoughts, and yet betrayed in his ambitious expectation of so perpetuating them.

The slow influences of the elements have been incessantly, though insensibly, obliterating what the
chisel had ploughed into the solid marble, till at
length nothing remains but a mockery of skeleton
letters, so unlike their pristine forms, so unable to
explain their own meaning, that you might as well
seek among the human relics in a charnel-vault the
resemblance of the once living personages—or in-
voke the dead bones to tell their own history—as
question those dumb rocks concerning the records
engraven on them.

The passage just quoted shows the state of alpha-
betical writing in the age of Job, and according to
the best commentators, he describes three modes of
exercising it: —"O that my words were now written—traced out in characters—in a book composed
of palm-leaves or on a roll of linen! O that they were
engraven with a pen of iron on tablets of lead, or in-
dented in the solid rock to endure to the end of
time!"

Arguing against the perverse sophistry of his
friends that he must have been secretly a wicked

man, *because* such awful calamities, which they construed into divine judgments, had befallen him. So just does he hold his integrity that, not only with passing words liable to be forgotten as soon as spoken, does he maintain it, but by every mode that could give his expressions publicity and ensure them perpetuity, he longs that his confidence in God to vindicate him might be recorded, whatever might be the issue of those evils to himself, even though he were brought down by them to death and corruption, descending not only with sorrow, but with ignominy to the grave. For saith he, "I know that my Redeemer liveth, and that He shall stand at the latter day on the earth; and though after my skin worms destroy this body, yet in my flesh shall I see God, whom I shall see for myself, and mine eyes shall behold though my reins be consumed within me."

Had these words of the patriarch been indeed "engraven with a pen of iron on the rock for ever," yet without some more certain medium of transmission to posterity, they would have been unknown at this day or only speaking in the desert with the voice of silence, which no eye could interpret, no mind could hear.

But, being inscribed on materials as frail as the leaves in my hand, yet capable of infinitely multiplied transcription, they can never be lost, for though the giant characters enchased in everlasting flint would ere now have been worn down by the perpetual foot of time, yet, committed with feeble ink to perishable paper, liable "to be crushed before the moth," or destroyed by the touch of fire or water, the good man's hope can never fail, even on earth. It was "a hope full of immortality," and still through all ages and in all lands, while the sun and moon endure, it shall be said by people of every kindred and

nation, and in every tongue spoken under heaven,
"I know that my Redeemer liveth."

QUESTIONS — 1. What evidence does the author use as proof
that writing was known in Egypt at the time of Moses? 2. According to the author, why is fragile paper more capable of
transmitting words to future generations than inscriptions chis-
eled in stone? 3. What materials for writing were known to Job?

SPELL AND DEFINE — (1) emancipation, memorials; (2) allusion, genealogy, chronicles, citizenship, oriental; (3) documents,
practically, acquainted, testimonies, frontlets, caviling, commentators, paradox; (5) extraordinary, composition, dramatic,
philosophy, patriarchal; (7) credence, fragments, undecipherable, wilderness, depositories, perpetuating; (8) incessantly,
obliterating.

LESSON XXI (21)

Criminality of Dueling—NOTT

NOTE—Alexander Hamilton, American statesman and found-
ing father, was challenged to a duel by Aaron Burr because of
some remarks Hamilton had allegedly made at a dinner party.
Although Hamilton opposed the practice of dueling, he accepted Burr's challenge, fearing that a refusal would result in
his loss of reputation and political influence. The men met early
on July 11, 1804—in the very place where Hamilton's eldest son
had died in a duel three years earlier—and Burr's bullet killed
Hamilton, leaving his wife with seven children and heavy debts.

Hamilton yielded to the force of an imperious
custom, and yielding, he sacrificed a life in which all
had an interest. And he is lost, lost to his country,
lost to his family, lost to us. For this rash act,
because he disclaimed it and was penitent, I forgive
him. But there are those whom I cannot forgive. I
mean not his antagonist, over whose erring steps, if

there be tears in heaven, a pious mother looks down and weeps.

If he be capable of feeling, he suffers already all that humanity can suffer—suffers, and wherever he may flee, will suffer with the poignant recollection of having taken the life of one who was too magnanimous in return to attempt his own. If he had known this, it surely might have paralyzed his arm while he pointed, at so incorruptible a bosom, the instrument of death. Does he know this now, his heart, if it be not adamant, must soften; if it be not ice, it must melt. . . . But on this article I forbear. Stained with blood as he is, if he be penitent, I forgive him; and if he be not, before these altars, where all of us appear as suppliants, I wish not to excite your vengeance, but rather, in behalf of an object rendered wretched and pitiable by crime, to wake your prayers.

But I have said and I repeat it, there are those whom I cannot forgive. I cannot forgive that minister at the altar, who has hitherto forborne to remonstrate on this subject. I cannot forgive that public prosecutor, who, intrusted with the duty of avenging his country's wrongs, has seen these wrongs and taken no measures to avenge them. I cannot forgive that judge upon the bench or that governor in the chair of state, who has lightly passed over such offenses. I cannot forgive the public, in whose opinion the duelist finds a sanctuary. I cannot forgive you, my brethren, who till this late hour have been silent while successive murders were committed.

No, I cannot forgive you, that you have not in common with the freemen of this state raised your voice to the powers that be and loudly and explicitly demanded an execution of your laws, demanded this in a manner, which, if it did not reach the ear of government, would at least have reached the heavens, and have pleaded your excuse before the God that filleth them—in whose presence as I stand, I should not feel myself innocent of the blood that crieth against us, had I been silent. But I have not been silent. Many of you who hear me are my witnesses. The walls of yonder temple, where I have heretofore addressed you, are my witnesses of how freely I have spoken against this subject in the presence both of those who have violated the laws and of those whose indispensable duty it is to see the laws executed on those who violate them.

I enjoy another opportunity, and would to God, I might be permitted to approach for once the last scene of death. Would to God, I could there assemble on the one side the disconsolate mother with her seven fatherless children, and on the other those who administer the justice of my country. Could I do this, I would point them to these sad objects. I would entreat them, by the agonies of bereaved fondness, to listen to the widow's heartfelt groans; to mark the orphan's sighs and tears; and having done this, I would uncover the breathless corpse of Hamilton; I would lift from his gaping wound his bloody mantle; I would hold it up to heaven before them; and I would ask, in the name of God, I would ask, whether at the sight of it they felt no compunction. You who have hearts of pity; you who have experienced the anguish of dissolving friendship; who have wept, and still weep over the moldering ruins of departed kindred, you can enter into this reflection.

O thou disconsolate widow! robbed, so cruelly robbed, and in so short a time, both of a husband and a son! What must be the plenitude of thy suffering! Could we approach thee, gladly would we drop the tear of sympathy, and pour into thy bleeding bosom the balm of consolation! But how could we

comfort her whom God hath not comforted! To His
throne let us lift up our voices and weep. O God! if
thou art still the widow's husband, and the father of
the fatherless; if, in the fullness of thy goodness,
there be yet mercy in store for miserable mortals,
pity, O pity this afflicted mother, and grant that her
hapless orphans may find a friend, a benefactor, a
father in thee!

QUESTIONS — 1. Why does the writer forgive Hamilton?
2. Whom does he not forgive—and why? 3. Describe the scene
that the writer would like to set up and use as a convincing
argument against dueling. 4. In the last paragraph the style
changes as the writer concludes his oration. This dramatic style
of oratory is no longer used. Read it aloud and imagine the effect it would have had on a contemporary audience.

SPELL AND DEFINE — (1) sacrificed; (2) magnanimous, penitent; (3) remonstrate, prosecutor; (4) explicitly; (5) disconsolate,
bereaved, reflection; (6) consolation, orphans.

LESSON XXII (22)

Character of Napoleon Bonaparte
PHILLIPS

NOTE—The author of this piece, Wendell Phillips (1811–1884), was an important abolitionist and reformer and one of the most eloquent orators of the day. He sacrificed social status and a prospective political career to devote himself to the unpopular cause of the slave. During the last decade of his life, he was active on the lyceum circuits, giving popular lectures on non-controversial subjects. This lecture on Napoleon displays his oratory skills.

He is fallen! We may now pause before that splendid prodigy, which towered among us like some ancient ruin whose frown terrified the glance its magnificence attracted. Grand, gloomy, and peculiar, he sat upon the throne a sceptered hermit, wrapt in the solitude of his own originality. A mind, bold, independent, and decisive; a will, despotic in its dictates; an energy that distanced expedition, and a conscience pliable to every touch of interest, marked the outline of this extraordinary character, the most extraordinary, perhaps, that in the annals of this world ever rose or reigned or fell. Flung into life in the midst of a revolution that quickened every energy of a people who acknowledge no superior, he commenced his course, a stranger by birth and a scholar by charity. With no friend but his sword and no fortune but his talents, he rushed in the list where rank, and wealth, and genius had arrayed themselves, and competition fled from him as from the glance of destiny.

He knew no motive but interest; acknowledged no criterion but success; he worshiped no God but ambition, and with an eastern devotion he knelt at the shrine of his idolatry. Subsidiary to this, there was no creed that he did not profess, there was no opinion that he did not promulgate: in the hope of a dynasty, he upheld the crescent; for the sake of a divorce, he bowed before the cross. The orphan of St. Louis, he became the adopted child of the republic; and with a parricidal ingratitude, on the ruins both of the throne and tribune, he reared the throne of his despotism. A professed Catholic, he imprisoned the pope; a pretended patriot, he impoverished the country; and, in the name of Brutus, he grasped without remorse, and wore without shame, the diadem of the Caesars!

Through this pantomime of policy, fortune played the clown to his caprices. At his touch, crowns crumbled, beggars reigned, systems vanished, the wildest theories took the color of his whim, and all that was venerable, and all that was novel, changed places with the rapidity of a drama. Even apparent defeat assumed the appearance of victory: his flight from Egypt confirmed his destiny; ruin itself only elevated him to empire. But if his fortune was great, his genius was transcendent; decision flashed upon his councils; and it was the same to decide and to perform. To *inferior* intellects his combinations appeared perfectly impossible, his plans perfectly impracticable; but, in *his* hands, simplicity marked their development, and success vindicated their adoption. His person partook the character of his mind: if the *one* never yielded in the cabinet, the *other* never bent in the field. Nature had no obstacle that he did not surmount; space no opposition he did not spurn; and whether amid Alpine rocks, Arabian sands, or Polar snows, he seemed proof against peril and empowered with ubiquity.

The whole continent trembled at beholding the

audacity of his designs and the miracle of their execution. Skepticism bowed to the prodigies of his
performance; romance assumed the air of history,
nor was there aught too incredible for belief or too
fanciful for expectation, when the world saw a subaltern of Corsica waving his imperial flag over her
most ancient capitals. All the visions of antiquity
became commonplaces in his contemplation: kings
were his people; nations were his outposts; and he
disposed of courts, and crowns, and camps, and
churches, and cabinets, as if they were titular digni-
taries of the chessboard. Amid all these changes he
stood immutable as adamant.

It mattered little whether in the field or in the
drawing-room; with the mob or the levee; wearing
the jacobin bonnet or the iron crown; banishing a
Braganza, or espousing a Hapsburg; dictating
peace on a raft to the Czar of Russia or contemplating defeat at the gallows of Leipsig; he was still
the same military despot.

In this wonderful combination, his affectations of
literature must not be omitted. The jailer of the
press, he affected the patronage of letters; the pro-
scriber of books, he encouraged philosophy; the per-
secutor of authors and the murderer of printers, he
yet pretended to the protection of learning; the
assassin of Palm, the silencer of de Stael, and the
denouncer of Kotzebue, he was the friend of David,
the benefactor of De Lille, and sent his academic
prize to the philosopher of England.

Such a medley of contradictions, and at the same
time such an individual consistency, were never
united in the same character. A royalist; a republican and an emperor; a Mohammedan; a Catholic and
a patron of the synagogue; a subaltern and a sovereign; a traitor and a tyrant; a Christian and an in-
fidel; he was, through all his vicissitudes, the same

stern, impatient, inflexible original; the same mysterious, incomprehensible self; the man without a model and without a shadow.

QUESTIONS — 1. To appreciate and understand fully this oration, you would have to be well acquainted with the details of Napoleon's career. His accomplishments are referred to, but not explained. What areas, besides the military, did Napoleon influence? 2. Phillips calls Napoleon a "medley of contradictions." What were some of these contradictions? 3. What was Napoleon's ruling passion? 4. Does Phillips present Napoleon as someone to admire? On what do you base your answer?

SPELL AND DEFINE — (1) magnificence, extraordinary; (2) criterion, parricidal, promulgate; (3) caprices, vindicated; (4) audacity, adamant; (5) despot; (6) affectations, denouncer; (7) inflexible, incomprehensible.

LESSON XXIII (23)

The Death of the Flowers
W. C. BRYANT

NOTE—The English romantic poet, William Wordsworth had the greatest influence on Bryant. Like Wordsworth and other romantic poets, Bryant found moral and spiritual significance in nature.

The melancholy days are come,
    The saddest of the year,
Of wailing winds, and naked woods,
    And meadows, brown and sear.
Heaped in the hollows of the grove,
    The withered leaves lie dead;
They rustle to the eddying gust,
    And to the rabbit's tread.

The robbin and the wren have flown,
    And from the shrub the jay,
And from the wood-top calls the crow
    Through all the gloomy day.

Where are the flowers, the fair young flowers,
    That lately sprang and stood
In brighter light and softer airs,
    A beauteous sisterhood?
Alas! they all are in their graves;
    The gentle race of flowers
Are lying in their lowly beds,
    With the fair and good of ours.
The rain is falling where they lie,
    But the cold November rain
Calls not from out the gloomy earth
    The lovely ones again.

The wallflower and the violet,
    They perished long ago,
And the brier-rose and the orchis died
    Amid the *summer's* glow;
But on the hill, the golden rod,
    And the aster in the wood,
And the yellow sun-flower by the brook
    In autumn beauty stood,
Till fell the frost from the clear, cold heaven,
    As falls the plague on men,
And the brightness of their smile was gone
    From upland, glade, and glen.

And *now*, when comes the calm, mild day,
    As still such days will come,
To call the squirrel and the bee
    From out their winter home;
When the sound of dropping nuts is heard,
    Though all the trees are still,

And twinkle in the smoky light
   The waters of the rill,
The south wind searches for the flowers
   Whose fragrance late he bore,
And sighs to find them in the wood
   And by the stream no more.

And then I think of one, who in
   Her youthful beauty died,
The fair, meek blossom that grew up
   And faded by my side;
In the cold, moist earth we laid her,
   When the forest cast the leaf,
And we wept that one so lovely
   Should have a life so brief:
Yet not unmeet it was that one,
   Like that young friend of ours,
So gentle and so beautiful,
   Should perish with the flowers.

QUESTIONS — 1. What season of the year is Bryant describing? 2. In stanza three he shows that various flowers died at different times. According to Bryant, which flowers died in the spring? Which in the summer? Which in the fall? Was he accurate? 3. What analogy does he make in the final stanza?

LESSON XXIV (24)

The Splendor of War—CHALMERS

NOTE—"The McGuffey READERS were most consistent in opposing war. . . . In contrast to most competing textbooks. . . . [the READERS did not contain] lots of lessons describing brave soldiers and military heroes." (Lindberg, p. 243.)

The first great obstacle to the extinction of war is the way by which the heart of man is carried off from its barbarities and its horrors, by the splendor of its deceitful accompaniments. There is a feeling of the sublime in contemplating the shock of armies, just as there is in contemplating the devouring energy of a tempest. And this so elevates and engrosses the whole man, that his eye is blind to the tears of bereaved parents, and his ear is deaf to the piteous moan of the dying, and the shriek of their desolated families.

There is a gracefulness in the picture of a youthful warrior burning for distinction on the field, and lured by this generous aspiration to the deepest of the animated throng, where, in the fell work of death, the opposing sons of valor struggle for a remembrance and a name. And this side of the picture is so much the exclusive object of our regard, as to disguise from our view the mangled carcasses of the fallen and the writhing agonies of the hundreds and the hundreds more who have been laid on the cold ground and left to languish and to die.

There no eye pities them. No sister is there to weep over them. There no gentle hand is present to ease the dying posture or bind up the wounds, which, in the maddening fury of the combat, had been given and received by the children of one common father. There death spreads its pale ensigns over every countenance, and when night comes on, and darkness gathers around them, how many a despairing wretch must take up with the bloody field as the untented bed of his last sufferings, without one friend to bear the message of tenderness to his distant home, without one companion to close his eyes.

I avow it. On every side of me I see causes at work, which go to spread a most delusive coloring over war, to remove its shocking barbarities to the background of our contemplations altogether. I see it in the history which tells me of the superb appearance of the troops and the brilliancy of their successive charges. I see it in the poetry which lends the magic of its numbers to the narrative of blood, and transports its many admirers, as, by its images and its figures and its nodding plumes of chivalry, it throws its treacherous embellishments over a scene of legalized slaughter.

I see it in the music which represents the progress of the battle; and where, after being inspired by the trumpet-notes of preparation, the whole beauty and tenderness of a drawing-room are seen to bend over the sentimental entertainment; nor do I hear the utterance of a single sigh to interrupt the death-tones of the thickening contest and the moans of the wounded men as they fade away upon the ear and sink into lifeless silence.

All, all goes to prove what strange and half-sighted creatures we are. Were it not so, war could never have been seen in any other aspect than that of unmingled hatefulness. I can look to nothing but to the progress of Christian sentiment upon earth, to arrest the strong current of its popular and prevailing partiality for war.

Then only will an imperious sense of duty lay the

check of severe principle, on all the subordinate tastes and faculties of our nature. Then will glory be reduced to its right estimate, and the wakeful benevolence of the gospel, chasing away every spell, will be devoted to simple but sublime enterprises for the good of the species.

QUESTIONS — 1. According to the writer, what stands in the way of the elimination of war? 2. What realities do the above "deceitful accompaniments" hide? 3. What makes death on the battlefield so terrible? 4. What does the writer view as the only hope for stopping the popularity of war? 5. Why is this essay entitled "The Splendor of War"?

SPELL AND DEFINE — (1) obstacle, extinction, barbarities, accompaniments, contemplating, devouring, engrosses; (2) gracefulness, animated, remembrance, carcasses, languish; (3) combat, ensigns; (4) brilliancy, treacherous, embellishments, legalized.

LESSON XXV (25)

The Spider and the Fly
MARY HOWITT

NOTE—Drawing lessons from the realm of nature is an ancient art that continues to be practiced by poets, philosophers, and teachers. In this lighthearted poem the drama of life among the wild creatures is presented in human words to reveal to humans their own foibles.

"Will you walk into my parlor?"
    said a spider to a fly,
"'Tis the prettiest little parlor
    that ever you did spy.
The way into my parlor is up a winding stair,

And I have many pretty things
    to show when you are there."
"Oh no, no," said the little fly,
    "to ask me is in vain,
For who goes up your winding stair
    can ne'er come down again."

"I'm sure you must be weary
    with soaring up so high;
Will you rest upon my little bed?"
    said the spider to the fly.
"There are pretty curtains drawn around,
    the sheets are fine and thin;
And if you like to rest awhile,
    I'll snugly tuck you in."
"Oh no, no," said the little fly,
    "for I've often heard it said,
They *never, never, wake* again,
    who sleep upon *your* bed!"

Said the cunning spider to the fly,
    "Dear friend, what shall I do,
To prove the warm affection
    I've always felt for you?
I have within my pantry,
    good store of all that's nice;
I'm sure you're very welcome;
    will you please to take a slice?"
"Oh no, no!" said the little fly,
    "kind sir, that cannot be;
I've *heard* what's in your pantry,
    and I do not *wish* to *see*."

"Sweet creature!" said the spider,
    "you're witty and you're wise,
How handsome are your gauzy wings,
    how brilliant are your eyes!

I have a little looking-glass upon my parlor shelf,
If you'll step in one moment, dear,
    you shall behold yourself."
"I thank you, gentle sir," said she,
    "for what you're pleased to say,
And bidding you good morning *now*,
    I'll call *another* day."

The spider turned him round about,
    and went into his den,
For well he knew the silly fly
    would soon be back again:
So he wove a subtile web, in a little corner, sly,
And set his table ready to dine upon the fly.
Then he went out to his door again,
    and merrily did sing,
"Come hither, hither, pretty fly,
    with the pearl and silver wing:
Your robes are green and purple,
    there's a crest upon your head;
Your eyes are like the diamond bright,
    but mine are dull as lead."

Alas, alas! how very soon this silly little fly,
Hearing his wily, flattering words,
    came slowly flitting by;
With buzzing wings she hung aloft,
    then near and nearer drew,
Thinking only of her brilliant eyes,
    and green and purple hue;
Thinking only of her crested head—
    poor foolish thing! At last,
Up jumped the cunning spider,
    and fiercely held her fast.

He dragged her up his winding stair,
    into his dismal den,

Within his little parlor;
    but she ne'er came out again!
And now, my dear young friends,
    who may this story read,
To idle, silly, flattering words,
    I pray you, ne'er give heed;
Unto an evil counselor,
    close heart, and ear, and eye.
And take a lesson from the tale
    of the Spider and the Fly.

QUESTIONS — 1. What enticements was the fly able to resist?
2. What enticement was the fly unable to resist? 3. What moral
is to be drawn from this little narrative poem?

SPELL AND DEFINE — (1) parlor; (2) soaring; (3) affection;
(4) gauzy, brilliant; (5) merrily, diamond; (6) flattering, fiercely;
(7) dismal.

LESSON XXVI (26)

The Journey of a Day—DR. JOHNSON

NOTE—Samuel Johnson is one of the most quoted English
authors and conversationalists. His monumental *Dictionary of
the English Language* (1755) provided the basis for all diction-
aries that were to follow. Besides his essays of literary criticism,
he also wrote moralistic essays—"The Journey of a Day," being
an example of the latter.

Obidah, the son of Abensina, left the inn early in
the morning and pursued his journey through the
plains of Hindostan. He was fresh and vigorous
with rest; he was animated with hope; he was in-
cited by desire. He walked swiftly forward over the
valleys and saw the hills gradually rising before
him.

As he passed along his ears were delighted with the morning song of the bird of paradise; he was fanned by the last flutters of the sinking breeze and sprinkled with dew by groves of spices. He sometimes contemplated the towering height of the oak, monarch of the hills; and sometimes caught the gentle fragrance of the primrose, eldest daughter of the spring. All his senses were gratified, and all care was banished from his heart.

Thus he went on till the sun approached his meridian, and the increasing heat preyed upon his strength. He then looked round about him for some more commodious path. He saw, on his right hand, a grove that seemed to wave its shades as a sign of invitation. He entered it and found the coolness and verdure irresistibly pleasant. He did not, however, forget whither he was traveling, but found a narrow way bordered with flowers, which appeared to have the same direction with the main road and was pleased that, by this happy experiment, he had found means to unite pleasure with business and to gain the rewards of diligence without suffering its fatigues.

He, therefore, still continued to walk for a time without the least remission of his ardor, except that he was sometimes tempted to stop by the music of the birds, whom the heat had assembled in the shade, and sometimes amused himself with plucking the flowers that covered the banks on either side or the fruits that hung upon the branches. At last the green path began to decline from its first tendency and to wind among the hills and thickets, cooled with fountains, and murmuring with waterfalls.

Here Obidah paused for a time and began to consider whether it were longer safe to forsake the known and common track, but remembering that the heat was now in its greatest violence and that the plain was dusty and uneven, he resolved to pursue the new path, which he supposed only to make a few meanders in compliance with the varieties of the ground and to end at last in the common road.

Having thus calmed his solicitude, he renewed his pace, though he suspected he was not gaining ground. This uneasiness of his mind inclined him to lay hold on every new object and give way to every sensation that might soothe or divert him. He listened to every echo, he mounted every hill for a fresh prospect, he turned aside to every cascade, and pleased himself with tracing the course of a gentle river that rolled among the trees and watered a large region with innumerable circumvolutions.

In these amusements the hours passed away unaccounted. His deviations had perplexed his memory, and he knew not towards what point to travel. He stood pensive and confused, afraid to go forward lest he should go wrong, yet conscious that the time of loitering was now past. While he was thus tortured with uncertainty, the sky was overspread with clouds, the day vanished from before him, and a sudden tempest gathered round his head.

He was now roused by his danger to a quick and painful remembrance of his folly. He now saw how happiness is lost when ease is consulted. He lamented the unmanly impatience that prompted him to seek shelter in the grove and despised the petty curiosity that led him on from trifle to trifle. While he was thus reflecting, the air grew blacker, and a clap of thunder broke his meditation.

He now resolved to do what remained yet in his power—to tread back the ground which he had passed and try to find some outlet, where the wood might open into the plain. He prostrated himself upon the ground and commended his life to the Lord of nature. He rose with confidence and tranquility and pressed on with his saber in his hand, for the beasts of the desert were in motion, and on every hand were heard the mingled howls of rage and fear and ravage and expiration: all the horrors of darkness and solitude surrounded him. The winds roared in the woods, and the torrents tumbled from the hills.

Thus, forlorn and distressed, he wandered through the wild without knowing whither he was going or whether he was every moment drawing nearer to safety or to destruction. At length, not fear, but labor, began to overcome him. His breath grew short, and his knees trembled, and he was on the point of lying down in resignation to his fate, when he beheld through the brambles the glimmer of a taper. He advanced towards the light, and finding that it proceeded from the cottage of a hermit, he called humbly at the door and obtained admission. The old man set before him such provisions as he had collected for himself, on which Obidah fed with eagerness and gratitude.

When the repast was over, "Tell me," said the hermit, "by what chance thou hast been brought hither: I have been now twenty years an inhabitant of this wilderness, in which I never saw a man before." Obidah then related the occurrences of his journey without any concealment or palliation.

"Son," said the hermit, "let the errors and follies, the dangers and escapes of this day sink deep into thy heart. Remember, my son, that human life is the journey of a day. We rise in the morning of youth, full of vigor and full of expectation; we set forward with spirit and hope, with gaiety and with diligence, and travel on a while in the straight road of piety, towards the mansions of rest. In a short time we remit our fervor and endeavor to find some mitigation of our duty and some more easy means of obtaining the same end.

"We then relax our vigor, and resolve no longer to be terrified with crimes at a distance, but rely upon our own constancy and venture to approach what we resolve never to touch. We thus enter the bowers of ease and repose in the shades of security. Here the heart softens and vigilance subsides: we are then willing to inquire whether another advance cannot be made and whether we may not, at least, turn our eyes upon the gardens of pleasure. We approach them with scruple and hesitation; we enter them, but enter timorous and trembling, and always hope to pass through them without losing the road of virtue, which we, for a while, keep in our sight, and to which we propose to return.

"But temptation succeeds temptation, and one compliance prepares us for another. We, in time, lose the happiness of innocence and solace our disquiet with sensual gratifications. By degrees we let fall the remembrance of our original intention and quit the only adequate object of rational desire. We entangle ourselves in business, immerge ourselves in luxury, and rove through the labyrinths of inconstancy, till the darkness of old age begins to invade us and disease and anxiety obstruct our way. We then look back upon our lives with horror, with sorrow, and with repentance, and wish, but too often vainly wish, that we had not forsaken the paths of virtue.

"Happy are they, my son, who shall learn from thy example not to despair, but shall remember that, though the day is past and their strength is wasted, there yet remains one effort to be made; that reformation is never hopeless, nor sincere endeavors ever unassisted; that the wanderer may at length return, after all his errors; and that he,

who implores strength and courage from above,
shall find danger and difficulty give way before him.
Go now, my son, to thy repose, commit thyself to
the care of Omnipotence, and when the morning
calls again to toil, begin anew thy journey and thy
life."

QUESTIONS — 1. Why did Obidah leave the path he was on?
2. What led him away from the direction of his destination?
3. As the storm gathered around him, Obidah realizes the principle that underlay his problem. What was it? (See paragraph
eight) 4. To what did the hermit compare the troubles of
Obidah's journey?

SPELL AND DEFINE — (1) animated; (7) deviations, loitering;
(9) tranquility;   (10) resignation;   (11) hermit;   (13) timorous;
(14) labyrinths, inconstancy.

LESSON XXVII (27)

Portrait of a Patriarch—ADDISON

NOTE—This lesson, which is taken primarily from the book of
Job, is introduced by the English essayist Joseph Addison.
Addison's fame rests primarily on his contributions to the two
periodicals, *The Tatler* and *The Spectator*. In "Portrait of a
Patriarch," Job answers his critics by describing his character
and conduct before his days of affliction.

Selections from Job 29-31

I cannot forbear making an extract of several
passages, which I have always read with great
delight in the book of Job. It is the account which
that holy man gives of his behavior in the days of
his prosperity, and, if considered only as a human
composition, is a finer picture of a charitable and

good-natured man than is to be met with in any other author.

"Oh that I were as in months past, as in the days when God preserved me; when his candle shined upon my head, and when, by his light, I walked through darkness; when the Almighty was yet with me; when my children were about me; when I washed my steps with butter, and the rock poured out rivers of oil.

"When the ear heard me, then it blessed me; and when the eye saw me, it gave witness to me; because I delivered the poor that cried, and the fatherless, and him that had none to help him. The blessing of him that was ready to perish came upon me; and I caused the widow's heart to sing for joy. I was eyes to the blind, and feet was I to the lame; I was a father to the poor; and the cause which I knew not I searched out.

"Did not I weep for him that was in trouble? Was not my soul grieved for the poor? Let me be weighed in an even balance that God may know mine integrity. If I did despise the cause of my man servant or of my maid servant, when they contended with me, what then shall I do when God riseth up? and when he visiteth, what shall I answer him? Did not he that made me make him also?

"If I have withheld the poor from their desire, or have caused the eyes of the widow to fail, or have eaten my morsel myself alone, and the fatherless hath not eaten thereof; if I have seen any perish for want of clothing, or any poor without covering; if his loins have not blessed me, and if he were not warmed with the fleece of my sheep; if I have lifted up my hand against the fatherless, when I saw my help in the gate; then let mine arm fall from my shoulderblade, and mine arm be broken from the bone.

"I rejoiced not at the destruction of him that
hated me, nor lifted up myself when evil found him;
neither have I suffered my mouth to sin, by wishing
a curse to his soul. The stranger did not lodge in the
street; but I opened my doors to the traveler. If my
land cry against me, and the furrows thereof complain; if I have eaten the fruits thereof without
money, or have caused the owners thereof to lose
their life; let thistles grow instead of wheat, and
cockle instead of barley."

QUESTIONS — 1. What is gained by having a brief introduc-
tion by Addison? 2. How is Job's character revealed? 3. To
understand the setting of Job's speech here and the two lessons
to follow, read Job 1 and 2.

SPELL AND DEFINE — (1) charitable; (3) perish, searched;
(4) contended; (5) morsel, fleece; (6) destruction, stranger, traveler, complain.

LESSON XXVIII (28)

Divine Providence—JOB

NOTE—Eliphaz, the first of three friends to reply to Job,
assumes that he would meet adversity more bravely than Job
and that he understands the reasons for affliction. Though there
is truth in his statements, he lacks kindness and sympathy. Job
later says of his friends, "Miserable comforters are ye all."
(Job 16:2)

Job 5

Call now, if there be any that will answer thee;
And to which of the saints wilt thou turn?
For wrath killeth the foolish man,
And envy slayeth the silly one.
I have seen the foolish taking root:

But suddenly I cursed his habitation.
His children are far from safety,
And they are crushed in the gate,
Neither is there any to deliver them.
Whose harvest the hungry eateth up
And taketh it even out of the thorns,
And the robber swalloweth up their substance.
Although affliction cometh not forth of the dust,
Neither doth trouble spring out of the ground:
Yet man is born unto trouble,
As the sparks fly upward.

I would seek unto God,
And unto God would I commit my cause:
Who doeth great things and unsearchable;
Marvelous things without number:
Who giveth rain upon the earth,
And sendeth waters upon the fields:
To set up on high those that be low;
That those which mourn may be exalted to safety.
He disappointeth the devices of the crafty,
So that their hands can not perform
      their enterprise:
He taketh the wise in their own craftiness:
And the counsel of the froward
      is carried headlong:
They meet with darkness in the daytime,
And grope in the noonday as in the night.
But he saveth the poor from the sword,
From their mouth, and from the hand
      of the mighty.
So the poor hath hope,
And iniquity stoppeth her mouth.

Behold! happy is the man whom God correcteth:
Therefore despise not thou the chastening
      of the Almighty:

For he maketh sore, and bindeth up:
He woundeth, and his hands make whole.
He shall deliver thee in six troubles:
Yea, in seven there shall no evil touch thee.
In famine, he shall redeem thee from death:
And in war, from the power of the sword.
Thou shalt be hid from the scourge of the tongue:
Neither shalt thou be afraid of destruction
    when it cometh.
At destruction and famine thou shalt laugh:
Neither shalt thou be afraid of the beasts
    of the earth.
For thou shalt be in league with the stones
    of the field:
And the beasts of the field shall be at peace
    with thee.
And thou shalt know that thy tabernacle
    shall be in peace;
And thou shalt visit thy habitation,
    and shalt not sin.
Thou shalt know also that thy seed shall be great,
And thine offspring as the grass of the earth.
Thou shalt come to thy grave in a full age,
Like as a shock of corn cometh in, in his season.
Lo! this, we have searched it, so it is;
Hear it, and know thou it for thy good.

QUESTIONS — 1. What does this well known passage mean: "Man is born unto trouble, as the sparks fly upward"? 2. How does Eliphaz say he would handle troubles? 3. Whom does Eliphaz think has brought affliction to Job? Whom does Job 1-2 reveal has brought Job's troubles?

SPELL AND DEFINE — (1) habitation, affliction; (2) unsearchable, crafty, enterprise, iniquity; (3) chastening, redeem, scourge, famine, tabernacle, offspring.

LESSON XXIX (29)

The Works of God—JOB

NOTE—In His answer to Job, God does not explain the reason
for Job's suffering. Neither does He answer the other philosophical questions raised by Job and his friends. He simply reveals
Himself. His answer teaches that it is more important to understand the wisdom and majesty of God than to understand all
the reasons behind divine providence.

Job 38:1-17

Then the Lord answered Job
    out of the whirlwind, and said,
Who is this that darkeneth counsel
By words without knowledge?
Gird up now thy loins like a man;
For I will demand of thee, and answer thou me.

  Where wast thou when I laid the foundations
    of the earth?
Declare, if thou hast understanding.
Who hath laid the measures thereof,
    if thou knowest?
Or who hath stretched the line upon it?
Whereupon are the foundations thereof fastened?
Or who laid the corner stone thereof,
When the morning stars sang together,
And all the sons of God shouted for joy?

  Or who shut up the sea with doors,
When it brake forth, as if it had issued
    out of the womb?
When I made the cloud the garment thereof,
And thick darkness a swaddling-band for it,
And brake up for it my decreed place,

And set bars and doors,
And said, Hitherto shalt thou come,
    but no further;
And here shall thy proud waves be stayed?

  Hast thou commanded the morning
    since thy days;
And caused the dayspring to know his place;
That it might take hold of the ends of the earth,
That the wicked might be shaken out of it?
It is turned as clay to the seal;
And they stand as a garment.
And from the wicked their light is withholden,
And the high arm shall be broken.

  Hast thou entered into the springs of the sea?
Or hast thou walked in the search of the depth?
Have the gates of death been opened unto thee?
Or hast thou seen the doors of the
    shadow of death?
Hast thou perceived the breadth of the earth?
Declare if thou knowest it all.

  Where is the way where light dwelleth?
And as for darkness, where is the place thereof,
That thou shouldest take it to the bound thereof,
And that thou shouldest know the paths
    to the house thereof?
Knowest thou it because thou wast then born?
Or because the number of thy days is great?

  Hast thou entered into the treasures of the
snow?
Or hast thou seen the treasures of the hail,
Which I have reserved against the time of trouble,
Against the day of battle and of war?

By what way is the light parted,
Which scattereth the east wind upon the earth?
Who hath divided a watercourse for the
    overflowing of waters;
Or a way for the lightning of thunder;
To cause it to rain on the earth, where no man is;
On the wilderness, wherein there is no man;
To satisfy the desolate and waste ground;
And to cause the bud of the tender herb
    to spring forth?

Job 39:19-25

Hast thou given the horse strength?
Hast thou clothed his neck with thunder?
Canst thou make him afraid as a grasshopper?
The glory of his nostrils is terrible.
He paweth in the valley, and rejoiceth
    in his strength;
He goeth out to meet the armed men.

He mocketh at fear, and is not affrighted;
Neither turneth he back from the sword.
The quiver rattleth against him,
The glittering spear and the shield.
He swalloweth the ground with
    fierceness and rage;
Neither believeth he that it is the sound
    of the trumpet.
He saith among the trumpets, Ha! ha!
And he smelleth the battle afar off,
The thunder of the captains, and the shouting.

QUESTIONS — 1. God answers Job by asking him questions. What does Job's inability to answer reveal about himself? About God? 2. God uses the language of poetry to ask scientific

questions. What figurative language is used to describe the
earth? The sea? Death? Snow?

SPELL   AND   DEFINE   —   (1) counsel;   (2) foundations;
(3) issued,   decreed;   (4) dayspring;   (5) perceived;   (7) reserved;
(8) wilderness, desolate; (9) grasshopper, rejoiceth; (10) quiver,
fierceness.

LESSON XXX (30)

External Appearance of England
EVERETT

NOTE—Alexander H. Everett (1790–1847) was a U.S. author,
diplomat, and editor of the *North American Review*. In this
essay he contrasts the "modern" urban England, which was ex-
periencing the Industrial Revolution, with the historic rural
England, which he symbolized by its architectural monuments.

Whatever may be the extent of the distress in
England or the difficulty of finding any remedies
for it, which shall be at once practicable and sufficient, it is certain that the symptoms of decline
have not displayed themselves on the surface. And
no country in Europe at the present day, probably
none that ever flourished at any preceding period of
ancient or of modern times, ever exhibited so
strongly the outward marks of general industry,
wealth, and prosperity.

The misery that exists, whatever it may be,
retires from public view, and the traveler sees no
traces of it except in the beggars—which are not
more numerous than they are on the continent—in
the courts of justice, and in the newspapers. On the
contrary, the impressions he receives from the objects that meet his view are almost uniformly agreeable.

He is pleased with the attention paid to his personal accommodation as a traveler, with the excellent roads and the conveniences of the public carriages and inns. The country everywhere exhibits the appearance of high cultivation, or else of wild and picturesque beauty. Even the unimproved lands are disposed with taste and skill, so as to embellish the landscape very highly, if they do not contribute, as they might, to the substantial comfort of the people.

From every eminence, extensive parks and grounds, spreading far and wide over hill and vale, interspersed with dark woods and variegated with bright waters, unroll themselves before the eye like enchanting gardens. And while the elegant constructions of the modern proprietors fill the mind with images of ease and luxury, the mouldering ruins that remain of former ages, of the castles and churches of their feudal ancestors, increase the interest of the picture by contrast and associate with it poetical and affecting recollections of other times and manners.

Every village seems to be the chosen residence of industry and her handmaids—neatness and comfort. In the various parts of the island, her operations present themselves under the most amusing and agreeable variety of forms. Sometimes her devotees are mounting to the skies in factories of innumerable stories in height, and sometimes diving in mines into the bowels of the earth, or dragging up drowned treasures from the bottom of the sea.

At one time the ornamented grounds of a wealthy proprietor seem to realize the fabled Elysium; and, again, as you pass in the evening through some village engaged in the iron manufacture, where a thousand forges are feeding at once their dark-red fires, and clouding the air with their volumes of smoke, you might think yourself, for a moment, a little too near some drearier residence.

The aspect of the cities is as various as that of the country. Oxford, in the silent, solemn grandeur of its numerous collegiate palaces, with their massy stone walls and vast interior quadrangles, seems like the deserted capital of some departed race of giants. This is the splendid sepulcher, where science, like the Roman Tarpeia, lies buried under the weight of gold that rewarded her ancient services, and where copious libations of the richest Port and Madeira, are daily poured out to her memory.

At Liverpool, on the contrary, all is bustle, brick and business. Everything breathes of modern times, everybody is occupied with the concerns of the present moment excepting one elegant scholar, who unites a singular resemblance to the Roman face and dignified person of our Washington, with the magnificent spirit and intellectual accomplishments of his own Italian hero.

At every change in the landscape, you fall upon monuments of some new race of men, among the number that have in their turn inhabited these islands. The mysterious monument of Stonehenge, standing remote and alone upon a bare and boundless heath, as much unconnected with the events of past ages as it is with the uses of the present, carries you back, beyond all historical records, into the obscurity of a wholly unknown period.

Perhaps the Druids raised it. But by what machinery could these half barbarians have wrought and moved such immense masses of rock? By what fatality is it, that, in every part of the globe, the most durable impressions that have been made upon its surface were the work of races now entirely extinct? Who were the builders of the pyramids and the massy monuments of Egypt and India?

Stonehenge will remain unchanged, when the banks of the Thames shall be as bare as Salisbury heath. But the Romans had something of the spirit of these primitive builders, and they left everywhere distinct traces of their passage.

Half the castles in Great Britain were founded, according to tradition, by Julius Caesar. And abundant vestiges remain, throughout the island, of Roman walls and forts and military roads. Most of their castles have, however, been built upon and augmented at a later period and belong, with more propriety, to the brilliant period of Gothic architecture. Thus the keep of Warwick dates from the time of Caesar, while the castle itself, with its lofty battlements, extensive walls and large enclosures, bears witness to the age when every Norman chief was a military despot within his own barony.

To this period belongs the principal part of the magnificent Gothic monuments, castles, cathedrals, abbeys, priories, and churches, in various stages of preservation and of ruin: some, like Warwick and Alnwick castles, like Salisbury cathedral and Westminster abbey, in all their original perfection; others, like Kenilworth and Canterbury, little more than a rude mass of earth and rubbish; and others again in the intermediate stages of decay, borrowing a sort of charm from their very ruin and putting on their dark-green robes of ivy to conceal the ravages of time, as if the luxuriant bounty of nature were purposely throwing a veil over the frailty and feebleness of art.

But the Norman castles and churches, with all their richness and sublimity, fell with the power of their owners at the rise of the Commonwealth. The Independents were levelers of substance as well as form; and the material traces they left of their existence are the ruins of what their predecessors had built. They too, had an architecture, but it was not in wood nor stone. It was enough for them to lay the foundation of the nobler fabric of civil liberty. The effects of the only change in society that has since occurred, are seen in the cultivated fields, the populous and thriving cities, the busy ports, and the general prosperous appearance of the country.

QUESTIONS — 1. How does Everett judge the industrial changes occurring in England? (This would have been the first half of the 19th century.) 2. Everett contrasts the cities of Oxford and Liverpool. What makes the differences? Do these same differences still exist? 3. How do the architectural structures reflect the history of the country?

SPELL AND DEFINE — (1) symptoms, exhibited, prosperity; (2) uniformly; (3) accommodation, picturesque; (4) enchanting, interspersed, feudal, recollections; (6) ornamented, forges; (7) quadrangle; (8) intellectual, accomplishments.

LESSON XXXI (31)

Character of the Puritan Fathers of New England—GREENWOOD

NOTE—In 1620 a group of about 100 Puritans, seeking religious freedom, set sail in the Mayflower for America. Anchoring off Cape Cod in November, they drew up the Mayflower Compact, the first agreement for self-government ever put in force in America. In December they sailed across Cape Cod Bay and established Plymouth, Massachusetts.

One of the most prominent features which distinguished our forefathers was their determined resistance to oppression. They seemed born and brought up for the high and special purpose of showing to the world that the civil and religious rights of man—the rights of self-government, of conscience, and independent thought—are not merely things to be talked of and woven into theories, but to be adopted with the whole strength and ardor of the mind, and felt in the profoundest recesses of the heart, and carried out into the general life, and made the foundation of practical usefulness and visible beauty and true nobility.

Liberty with them, was an object of too serious desire and stern resolve to be personified, allegorized, and enshrined. They made no goddess of it, as the ancients did: they had no time nor inclination for such trifling. They felt that liberty was the simple birthright of every human creature; they called it so; they claimed it as such; they reverenced and held it fast as the unalienable gift of the Creator, which was not to be surrendered to power nor sold for wages.

It was theirs, as men; without it, they did not esteem themselves men. More than any other privilege or possession, it was essential to their happiness, for it was essential to their original nature, and therefore they preferred it above wealth and ease and country. And that they might enjoy and exercise it fully, they forsook houses and lands and kindred, their homes, their native soil, and their fathers' graves.

They left all these. They left England, which, whatever it might have been called, was not to them a land of freedom. They launched forth on the pathless ocean, the wide, fathomless ocean, soiled not by the earth beneath and bounded, all round and above, only by heaven. And it seemed to them like that better and sublimer freedom, which their country knew not, but of which they had the conception and image in their hearts. And after a toilsome and painful voyage, they came to a hard and wintry coast, unfruitful and desolate, but unguarded and boundless. Its calm silence interrupted not the ascent of their prayers; it had no eyes to watch, no ears to hearken, no tongues to report of them. Here, again, there was an answer to their soul's desire, and they were satisfied and gave thanks. They saw that they were free, and the desert smiled.

I am telling an old tale, but it is one which must be told, when we speak of those men. It is to be added, that they transmitted their principles to their children, and that peopled by such a race, our country was always free. So long as its inhabitants were unmolested by the mother country in the exercise of their important rights, they submitted to the form of English government; but when those rights were invaded, they spurned even the form away.

This act was the revolution, which came of course, and spontaneously, and had nothing in it of the wonderful or unforeseen. The wonder would have been, if it had not occurred. It was, indeed, a

happy and glorious event, but by no means un-
natural; and I intend no slight to the revered actors
in the revolution, when I assert that their fathers
before them were as free as they—every whit as
free.

The principles of the revolution were not the suddenly acquired property of a few bosoms; they were
abroad in the land in the ages before. They had
always been taught, like the truths of the Bible.
They had descended from father to son, down from
those primitive days, when the pilgrim, established
in his simple dwelling and seated at his blazing fire,
piled high from the forest which shaded his door,
repeated to his listening children the story of his
wrongs and his resistance, and bade them rejoice,
though the wild winds and the wild beasts were
howling without, that they had nothing to fear from
great men's oppression.

Here were the beginnings of the revolution.
Every settler's hearth was a school of independence. The scholars were apt, and the lessons sank
deeply. And thus it came that our country was
always free; it could not be other than free.

As deeply seated as was the principle of liberty
and resistance to arbitrary power, in the breasts of
the Puritans, it was not more so than their piety and
sense of religious obligation. They were emphatically a people whose God was the Lord. Their form
of government was as strictly theocratical, if direct
communication be excepted, as was that of the
Jews; because it would be difficult to say where
there was any civil authority among them entirely
distinct from ecclesiastical jurisdiction.

Whenever a few of them settled a town, they immediately gathered themselves into a church; and
their elders were magistrates, and their code of laws
was the Pentateuch. These were forms, it is true,

but forms which faithfully indicated principles and feelings: for no people could have adopted such forms, who were not thoroughly imbued with the spirit and bent on the practice of religion.

God was their King; and they regarded Him as truly and literally so, as if He had dwelt in a visible palace in the midst of their state. They were His devoted, resolute, humble subjects; they undertook nothing which they did not beg of Him to prosper; they accomplished nothing without rendering to Him the praise; they suffered nothing without carrying up their sorrows to His throne; they ate nothing which they did not implore Him to bless.

Their piety was not merely external; it was sincere; it had the proof of a good tree in bearing good fruit; it produced and sustained a strict morality. Their tenacious purity of manners and speech obtained for them, in the mother country, their name of Puritans, which, though given in derision, was as honorable an appellation as was ever bestowed by man on man.

That there were hypocrites among them is not to be doubted; but they were rare. The men who voluntarily exiled themselves to an unknown coast and endured there every toil and hardship for conscience' sake, and that they might serve God in their own manner, were not likely to set conscience at defiance and make the services of God a mockery; they were not likely to be, neither were they, hypocrites. I do not know that it would be arrogating too much for them to say, that, on the extended surface of the globe, there was not a single community of men to be compared with them, in the respects of deep religious impressions and an exact performance of moral duty.

QUESTIONS — 1. What motivated the Puritans to leave England and to settle in the wilderness of America? 2. Accord-

ing to the author, what were the beginnings of the revolution?
3. When a few of them settled a town, how did they set up
government? 4. Why were there few hypocrites among them?

SPELL AND DEFINE — (1) personified, allegorized; (4) fathomless; (7) pilgrim; (9) ecclesiastical, jurisdiction; (10) indicated; (11) resolute, implore; (12) tenacious; (13) hypocrite.

LESSON XXXII (32)

The Steamboat Trial—ABBOTT

NOTE—More than any other invention, James Watt's improved steam engine (in the 1760's) contributed to the growth of
the Industrial Revolution. It quickly became the chief source of
power for transportation and industry. This key role explains
why references to the steam engine are not uncommon in the
McGuffey READERS.

The Bible everywhere conveys the idea that this
life is not our home, but a state of probation, that is,
of *trial and discipline*, which is intended to prepare
us for another. In order that all, even the youngest
of my readers, may understand what is meant by
this, I shall illustrate it by some familiar examples,
drawn from the actual business of life.

When a large steamboat is built, with the intention of having her employed upon the waters of a
great river, she must be *proved* before put to service. Before trial, it is somewhat doubtful whether
she will succeed. In the first place, it is not absolutely certain whether her machinery will work at
all. There may be some flaw in the iron or an imperfection in some part of the workmanship, which will
prevent the motion of her wheels. Or if this is not
the case, the power of the machinery may not be

sufficient to propel her through the water, with such force as to overcome the current. Or she may, when brought to encounter the rapids at some narrow passage in the stream, not be able to force her way against their resistance.

The engineer, therefore, resolves to try her in all these respects, that her security and her power may be properly *proved* before she is entrusted with her valuable cargo of human lives. He cautiously builds a fire under her boiler; he watches with eager interest the rising of the steam-gage and scrutinizes every part of the machinery as it gradually comes under the control of the tremendous power, which he is apprehensively applying.

With what interest does he observe the first stroke of the ponderous piston! And when at length the fastenings of the boat are let go, and the motion is communicated to the wheels, and the mighty mass slowly moves away from the wharf, how deep and eager an interest does he feel in all her movements and in every indication he can discover of her future success!

The engine, however, works imperfectly, as every one must on its first trial. And the object in this experiment is not to gratify idle curiosity by seeing that she will move, but to discover and remedy every little imperfection and to remove every obstacle which prevents more entire success. For this purpose, you will see our engineer examining, most minutely and most attentively, every part of her complicated machinery. The crowd on the wharf may be simply gazing on her majestic progress as she moves off from the shore, but the engineer is within, looking with faithful examination into all the minutia of the motion.

He scrutinizes the action of every lever and the friction of every joint. Here, he oils a bearing; there, he tightens a nut. One part of the machinery has too much play, and he confines it; another, too much friction, and he loosens it. Now, he stops the engine, now, reverses her motion, and again, sends the boat forward in her course. He discovers, perhaps, some great improvement of which she is susceptible, and when he returns to the wharf and has extinguished her fire, he orders from the machine-shop the necessary alteration.

The next day he puts his boat to the trial again, and she glides over the water more smoothly and swiftly than before. The jar which he had noticed is gone and the friction reduced; the beams play more smoothly, and the alteration which he has made produces a more equable motion in the shaft, or gives greater effect to the stroke of the paddles upon the water.

When at length her motion is such as to satisfy him upon the smooth surface of the river, he turns her course, we will imagine, toward the rapids to see how she will sustain a greater trial. As he increases her steam to give her power to overcome the new force with which she has to contend, he watches with eager interest her boiler, inspects the gage and the safety-valves, and, from her movements under the increased pressure of her steam, he receives suggestions for further improvements or for precautions which will insure greater safety.

These he executes, and thus he perhaps goes on for many days, or even weeks, trying and examining, for the purpose of improvement, every working of that mighty power, to which he knows hundreds of lives are soon to be entrusted. This now is probation—*trial for the sake of improvement.* And what are its results? Why, after this course has been thoroughly and faithfully pursued, this floating palace receives upon her broad deck and in her carpeted and curtained cabin, her four or five hundred passengers, who pour along in one long procession of happy groups, over the bridge of planks—father and son, mother and children, young husband and wife, all with implicit confidence, trusting themselves and their dearest interests to her power.

See her as she sails away! How beautiful and yet how powerful are all her motions! That beam glides up and down gently and smoothly in its grooves, and yet gentle as it seems, hundreds of horses could not hold it still. There is no apparent violence, but every movement is with irresistible power. How graceful is her form, and yet how mighty is the momentum with which she presses on her way!

Loaded with life, and herself the very symbol of life and power, she seems something ethereal, unreal, which, ere we look again, will have vanished away. And though she has within her bosom a furnace glowing with furious fires and a reservoir of death, the elements of most dreadful ruin and conflagration, of destruction the most complete, and agony the most unutterable, and though her strength is equal to the united energy of two thousand men, she restrains it all.

She was constructed by genius and has been *tried* and improved by fidelity and skill. One man governs and controls her, stops her and sets her in motion, turns her this way and that, as easily and certainly as the child guides the gentle lamb. She walks over the one hundred and sixty miles of her route without rest and without fatigue. And the passengers, who have slept in safety in their berths, with destruction by water without and by fire within, defended only by a plank from the one and by a sheet of copper from the other, land at the appointed time in safety.

My reader, you have within you susceptibilities

and powers, of which you have little present conception—energies, which are hereafter to operate in producing fullness of enjoyment or horrors of suffering, of which you now can form scarcely a conjecture. You are now on *trial*. God wishes you to prepare yourself for safe and happy action. He wishes you to look within, to examine the complicated movements of your hearts, to detect what is wrong, to modify what needs change, and to rectify every irregular motion.

You go out to try your moral powers upon the stream of active life, and then return to retirement to improve what is right and remedy what is wrong. Renewed opportunities of moral practice are given you, that you may go on from strength to strength, until every part of that complicated moral machinery, of which the human heart consists, will work as it ought to work, and is prepared to accomplish the mighty purposes for which your powers are designed. You are *on trial, on probation* now. You will enter upon *active service* in another world.

QUESTIONS — 1 This whole lesson is an analogy. What two things are being compared? 2. What aspects of the steamboat did the writer admire? Fear? 0. What is this writer's definition of probation?

SPELL AND DEFINE — (1) conveys, probation, illustrate; (2) workmanship, sufficient; (3) security; (4) communicate; (5) examination, minutia; (6) susceptible; (8) precautions; (10) grooves; (11) ethereal; (12) constructed, fatigue; (13) modify, rectify.

LESSON XXXIII (33)

The Righteous Never Forsaken
NEW YORK SPECTATOR

NOTE—If any story could be labeled "typical" of narratives written or selected by William McGuffey, this is surely one. It has all the key elements: a poor widow with needy children, kindnesses offered at the cost of self-denial, and finally, with the aid of remarkable circumstances, earthly reward.

It was Saturday night, and the widow of the Pine Cottage sat by her blazing fagots, with her five tattered children at her side, endeavoring by listening to the artlessness of their prattle, to dissipate the heavy gloom that pressed upon her mind. For a year her own feeble hand had provided for her helpless family, for she had no supporter: she thought of no friend in all the wide, unfriendly world around.

But that mysterious Providence, the wisdom of whose ways is above human comprehension, had visited her with wasting sickness, and her little means had become exhausted. It was now, too, midwinter, and the snow lay heavy and deep through all the surrounding forests, while storms still seemed gathering in the heavens, and the driving wind roared amid the neighboring pines and rocked her puny mansion.

The last herring smoked upon the coals before her; it was the only article of food she possessed, and no wonder her forlorn, desolate state brought up in her lone bosom all the anxieties of a mother, when she looked upon her children. And no wonder, forlorn as she was, if she permitted the heart swellings of despair to rise, even though she knew that He whose promise is to the widow and to the orphan, cannot forget His word.

Providence had, many years before, taken from her her eldest son, who went from his forest home to try his fortune on the high seas, since which she had heard no tidings of him; and, in her latter time, had, by the hand of death, deprived her of the companion and staff of her earthly pilgrimage, in the person of her husband. Yet to this hour she had been upborne; she had not only been able to provide for her little flock, but had never lost an opportunity of ministering to the wants of the miserable and destitute.

The indolent may well bear with poverty, while the ability to gain sustenance remains. The individual who has but his own wants to supply, may suffer with fortitude the winter of want; his affections are not wounded, his heart not wrung. The most desolate in populous cities may hope, for charity has not quite closed her hand and heart, and shut her eyes on misery.

But the industrious mother of helpless and depending children, far from the reach of human charity, has none of these to console her. And such a one was the widow of the Pine Cottage. But as she bent over the fire and took up the last scanty remnant of food, to spread before her children, her spirits seemed to brighten up, as by some sudden and mysterious impulse, and Cowper's beautiful lines came uncalled across her mind:

> Judge not the Lord by feeble sense,
> But trust him for his grace;
> Behind a frowning Providence
> He hides a smiling face.

The smoked herring was scarcely laid upon the table, when a gentle rap at the door and loud barking of a dog, attracted the attention of the family. The children flew to open it, and a weary traveler in tattered garments and apparently indifferent health, entered and begged a lodging and a mouthful of food. Said he, "It is now twenty-four hours since I tasted bread." The widow's heart bled anew as under a fresh complication of distresses, for her sympathies lingered not around her fireside. She hesitated not even now. Rest and a share of all she had she proffered to the stranger. "We shall not be forsaken," said she, "or suffer deeper for an act of charity."

The traveler drew near the board, but when he saw the scanty fare, he raised his eyes toward heaven with astonishment: "And is this *all* your store?" said he, "and a share of this do you offer to one you know not? Then never saw I *charity* before! But madam," said he, continuing, "do you not wrong your *children* by giving a part of your last mouthful to a stranger?"

"Ah," said the poor widow, and the teardrops gushed into her eyes as she said it, "I have a *boy*, a darling *son*, somewhere on the face of the wide world, unless heaven has taken him away, and I only act toward you, as I would that others should act toward him. God, who sent manna from heaven, can provide for us as he did for Israel. And how should I this night offend him, if my son should be a wanderer, destitute as you, and he should have provided for him a home, even poor as this, were I to turn you unrelieved away."

The widow ended, and the stranger springing from his seat, clasped her in his arms: "God indeed has provided your son a home and has given him wealth to reward the goodness of his benefactress: my mother! oh my mother!" It was her long lost son, returned to her bosom from the Indies. He had chosen that disguise that he might the more completely surprise his family; and never was surprise more perfect or followed by a sweeter cup of joy.

That humble residence in the forest was exchanged for one comfortable, and indeed beautiful, in the valley. The widow lived long with her dutiful son, in the enjoyment of worldly plenty, and in the delightful employments of virtue. And at this day the passer-by is pointed to the willow that spreads its branches above her grave.

QUESTIONS — 1. Why was the widow in a particularly distressing situation as this story begins? 2. How had the widow continued to treat the destitute, even though she herself was in constant need? 3. Why was the widow's offer to feed a poor stranger such a selfless act? 4. What brought the widow into "worldly plenty"?

SPELL AND DEFINE — (1) fagots, prattle; (2) mysterious, exhausted; (3) anxieties; (4) tidings; (5) indolent, populous; (6) console, remnant; (7) apparently; (9) wanderer, destitute; (10) benefactress; (11) residence.

LESSON XXXIV (34)

Religion the Only Basis of Society
CHANNING

NOTE—The prominent clergyman William Ellery Channing was pastor of the Federal Street Church in Boston for nearly forty years. He influenced such American writers as Ralph Waldo Emerson, Henry Wadsworth Longfellow, and James Russell Lowell.

Religion is a social concern for it operates powerfully on society, contributing, in various ways, to its stability and prosperity. Religion is not merely a private affair; the community is deeply interested in its diffusion; for it is the best support of the virtues and principles on which the social order rests. Pure

and undefiled religion is to do good; and it follows
very plainly that, if God be the Author and Friend
of society, then the recognition of him must enforce
all social duty and enlightened piety must give its
whole strength to public order.

Few men suspect, perhaps no man comprehends,
the extent of the support given by religion to every
virtue. No man, perhaps, is aware how much our
moral and social sentiments are fed from this fountain. How powerless conscience would become,
without the belief of a God. How palsied would be
human benevolence were there not the sense of a
higher benevolence to quicken and sustain it. How
suddenly the whole social fabric would quake, and
with what a fearful crash it would sink into hopeless
ruin were the ideas of a supreme Being, of account-
ableness, and of a future life to be utterly erased
from every mind.

And let men thoroughly believe that they are the
work and sport of chance, that no superior intelligence concerns itself with human affairs, that all
their improvements perish forever at death, that
the weak have no guardian and the injured no
avenger, that there is no recompense for sacrifices
to uprightness and the public good, that an oath is
unheard in heaven, that secret crimes have no witness but the perpetrator, that human existence has
no purpose and human virtue no unfailing friend,
that this brief life is everything to us and death is
total, everlasting extinction; once let them *thoroughly* abandon religion, and who can conceive or
describe the extent of the desolation which would
follow!

We hope, perhaps, that human laws and natural
sympathy would hold society together. As reason-
ably might we believe that were the sun quenched in
the heavens, *our* torches would illuminate, and *our*

fires quicken and fertilize the creation. What is there in human nature to awaken respect and tenderness, if man is the unprotected insect of a day? And what is he more, if atheism be true?

Erase all thought and fear of God from a community, and selfishness and sensuality would absorb the whole man. Appetite, knowing no restraint, and suffering, having no solace or hope, would trample in scorn on the restraints of human laws. Virtue, duty, principle would be mocked and spurned as unmeaning sounds. A sordid self-interest would supplant every feeling; and man would become, in fact, what the theory of atheism declares him to be—*a companion for brutes.*

QUESTIONS — 1. Why is religion a social concern? 2. What teachings of religion benefit society? (See paragraph three) 3. If mankind would completely forget God, what would become their obsessions? 4. Do you see any evidence today of Channing's prediction?

SPELL AND DEFINE — (1) community, diffusion; (2) comprehends, social; (3) intelligence, recompense, abandon; (4) illuminate; (5) sordid, supplant.

LESSON XXXV (35)

Love of Applause—HAWES

To be insensible to public opinion or to the estimation in which we are held by others, indicates anything, rather than a good and generous spirit. It is indeed the mark of a low and worthless character—devoid of principle and therefore devoid of shame. A young man is not far from ruin when he can say, without blushing, *I don't care what others think of me.*

But to have a proper regard to public opinion is one thing; to make that opinion our rule of action is quite another. The one we may cherish consistently with the purest virtue and the most unbending rectitude; the other we cannot adopt without an utter abandonment of principle and disregard of duty.

The young man whose great aim is to please, who makes the opinion and favor of others his rule and motive of action, stands ready to adopt any sentiments or pursue any course of conduct, however false and criminal, provided only that it be popular.

In every emergency his first question is, what will my companions, what will the world think and say of me, if I adopt this or that course of conduct? Duty, the eternal laws of rectitude, are not thought of. Custom, fashion, popular favor—these are the things that fill his entire vision and decide every question of opinion and duty.

Such a man can never be trusted for he has no integrity and no independence of mind to obey the dictates of rectitude. He is at the mercy of every casual impulse and change of popular opinion; and you can no more tell whether he will be right or wrong tomorrow, than you can predict the course of the wind or what shape the clouds will then assume.

And what is the usual consequence of this weak and foolish regard to the opinions of men? What the *end* of thus acting in compliance with custom in opposition to one's own convictions of duty? It is to lose the esteem and respect of the very men whom you thus attempt to please. Your defect of principle and hollow heartedness are easily perceived; and though the persons to whom you thus sacrifice your conscience may affect to commend your complaisance, you may be assured that inwardly they despise you for it.

Young men hardly commit a greater mistake than to think of gaining the esteem of others by yielding to their wishes, contrary to their own sense of duty. Such conduct is always morally wrong and rarely fails to deprive one, both of self respect and the respect of others.

It is very common for young men just commencing business, to imagine that if they would advance their secular interests, they must not be very scrupulous in binding themselves down to the strict rules of rectitude. They must conform to custom, and if in buying and selling they sometimes say the things that are not true and do the things that are not honest—why, their neighbors do the same; and verily, there is no getting along without it. There is so much competition and rivalry, that to be *strictly honest*, and yet succeed in business is out of the question.

Now if it were indeed so, I would say to a young man, then, quit your business. Better dig and beg too, than to tamper with conscience, sin against God, and lose your soul.

But, is it so? Is it necessary in order to succeed in business, that you should adopt a standard of morals more lax and pliable than the one placed before you in the Bible? Perhaps for a time, a rigid adherence to rectitude might bear hard upon you, but how would it be in the end? Possibly, your neighbor, by being less scrupulous than yourself, may invent a more expeditious way of acquiring a fortune. If he is willing to violate the dictates of conscience, to lie and cheat and trample on the rules of justice and honesty, he may, indeed, get the start of you and rise suddenly to wealth and distinction.

But would you envy him his riches or be willing to place yourself in his situation? Sudden wealth, especially when obtained by dishonest means, rarely fails of bringing with it sudden ruin. Those who acquire it, are of course beggared in their morals, and are often, very soon, beggared in property. Their riches are corrupted. And while they bring the curse of God on their immediate possessors, they usually entail misery and ruin upon their families.

If it be admitted then, that strict integrity is not always the shortest way to success, is it not the surest, the happiest, and the best? A young man of thorough integrity may, it is true, find it difficult in the midst of dishonest competitors and rivals, to start in his business or profession. But how long will it be before he will surmount every difficulty, draw around him patrons and friends, and rise in the confidence and support of all who know him?

What, if in pursuing this course, you should not, at the close of life, have so much money by a few hundred dollars? Will not a fair character, an approving conscience, and an approving God, be an abundant compensation for this little deficiency of riches?

O there is an hour coming, when one whisper of an approving mind, one smile of an approving God, will be accounted of more value than the wealth of a

thousand worlds like this. In that hour, my young
friends, nothing will sustain you but the consciousness of having been governed in life by worthy and
good principles.

QUESTIONS — 1. Is it desirable to disregard completely what
others think of you? 2. What is the result of basing all your
behavior on public opinion? 3. If you adopt as your rule of life
the honesty and justice taught in the Bible, what will be your
prospects for becoming wealthy? 4. At what time will you most
value your decision to live by a Biblically guided conscience?

SPELL AND DEFINE — (1) insensible, estimation; (2) consistently, rectitude, abandonment; (3) criminal; (4) companions;
(5) integrity, independence; (6) compliance, perceived; (8) commencing, scrupulous, neighbors, competition; (9) conscience;
(10) lax, pliable; (13) compensation.

LESSON XXXVI (36)

It Snows—MRS. S. J. HALE

NOTE—Left a widow with five children, Mrs. Sarah Josepha
Hale managed to support her family by writing. For forty years,
beginning in 1837, she was editor of *Godey's Lady's Book*. It
was her editorial campaign in that periodical that led President
Lincoln to issue a proclamation for a Thanksgiving Day in 1863.
(Lindberg, pp. 231, 232.)

"It snows!" cries the Schoolboy,
        "Hurrah!" and his shout
Is ringing through parlor and hall,
While swift as the wing of a swallow, he's out,
        And his playmates have answered his call;
It makes the heart leap but to witness their joy,
        Proud wealth has no pleasures, I trow,

Like the rapture that throbs in the pulse of the boy,
    As he gathers his treasures of snow;
Then lay not the trappings of gold on thine heirs,
While health, and the riches of nature, are theirs.

"It snows!" sighs the Sick Man, "Ah!" and his breath
    Comes heavy, as clogged with a weight;
While, from the pale aspect of nature in death,
    He turns to the blaze of his grate;
And nearer and nearer, his soft-cushioned chair
    Is wheeled toward the life-giving flame;
He dreads a chill puff of the snow-burdened air,
    Lest it wither his delicate frame;
Oh! small is the pleasure existence can give,
When the fear we shall die only proves that we live!

"It snows!" cries the Traveler, "Ho!" and the word
    Has quickened his steed's lagging pace;
The wind rushes by, but its howl is unheard
    Unfelt the sharp drift in his face;
For bright through the tempest
        his own home appeared,
    Ay, though leagues intervened, he can see:
There's the clear, glowing hearth,
        and the table prepared,
    And his wife with her babes at her knee;
Blest thought! how it lightens the grief-laden hour,
That those we love dearest are safe from its power!

"It snows!" cries the Belle,
        "Dear, how lucky!" and turns
    From her mirror to watch the flakes fall;
Like the first rose of summer,
        her dimpled cheek burns,
    While musing on sleigh-ride and ball:
There are visions of conquests, of splendor, and mirth,
    Floating over each drear winter's day;

But the tintings of Hope, on this storm-beaten earth,
   Will melt like the snowflakes away:
Turn, turn thee to Heaven, fair maiden, for bliss;
That world has a pure fount ne'er opened in this.

"It snows!" cries the Widow,
     "Oh God!" and her sighs
   Have stifled the voice of her prayer;
Its burden ye'll read in her tear-swollen eyes,
   On her cheek sunk with fasting and care.
'Tis night, and her fatherless ask her for bread;
   But "He gives the young ravens their food,"
And she trusts, till her dark hearth
     adds horror to dread,
   And she lays on her last chip of wood.
Poor sufferer! that sorrow thy God only knows;
'Tis a most bitter lot to be poor, when it snows!

QUESTIONS—How does the snow affect each of the following
people: 1. The school boy? 2. The sick man? 3. The traveler?
4. The belle? 5. The widow?

SPELL AND DEFINE — (1) rapture, treasures; (2) clogged,
aspect, delicate, existence; (3) lagging; (4) dimpled, splendor,
fount; (5) horror, sufferer.

LESSON XXXVII (37)

Tit for Tat—MISS EDGEWORTH

NOTE—There are few selections of humor in the READERS;
this domestic scene is one of the best. It was written by Maria
Edgeworth (1767-1849), an English woman who is chiefly
remembered for her children's stories which, while they teach a
lesson, are always lively.

Mrs. Bolingbroke. I wish I knew what was the
matter with me this morning. Why do you keep the
newspaper all to yourself, my dear?

Mr. Bolingbroke. Here it is for you, my dear. I
have finished it.

Mrs. B. I humbly thank you for giving it to me
when you have done with it. I hate stale news. Is
there anything in the paper? I cannot be at the trouble of hunting it.

Mr. B. Yes, my dear, there are the marriages of
two of our friends.

Mrs. B. Who? Who?

Mr. B. Your friend, the widow Nettleby, to her
cousin John Nettleby.

Mrs. B. Mrs. Nettleby? Dear! But why did you
tell me?

Mr. B. Because you asked me, my dear.

Mrs. B. Oh, but it is a hundred times pleasanter
to read the paragraph one's self. One loses all the
pleasure of the surprise by being told. Well, whose
was the other marriage?

Mr. B. Oh, my dear, I will not tell you. I will
leave you the pleasure of the surprise.

Mrs. B. But you see I cannot find it. How provoking you are, my dear! Do pray tell me.

Mr. B. Our friend, Mr. Granby.

Mrs. B. Mr. Granby? Dear! Why did you not make me guess? I should have guessed him directly. But why do you call him *our* friend? I am sure he is no friend of mine, nor ever was. I took an aversion to him, as you remember, the very first day I saw him. I am sure he is no friend of mine.

Mr. B. I am sorry for it, my dear, but I hope you will go and see Mrs. Granby.

Mrs. B. Not I, indeed, my dear. Who was she?

Mr. B. Miss Cooke.

Mrs. B. Cooke? But there are so many Cookes. Can't you distinguish her any way? Has she no Christian name?

Mr. B. Emma, I think. Yes, Emma.

Mrs. B. Emma Cooke? No, it cannot be my friend Emma Cooke, for I am sure she was cut out for an old maid.

Mr. B. This lady seems to me to be cut out for a good wife.

Mrs. B. May be so. I am sure I'll never go to see her. Pray, my dear, how came you to see so much of her?

Mr. B. I have seen very little of her, my dear. I only saw her two or three times before she was married.

Mrs. B. Then, my dear, how could you decide that she was cut out for a good wife? I am sure you could not judge of her by seeing her only two or three times, and before she was married.

Mr. B. Indeed, my love, that is a very just observation.

Mrs. B. I understand that compliment perfectly, and thank you for it, my dear. I must own I can bear anything better than irony.

Mr. B. Irony, my dear? I was perfectly in earnest.

Mrs. B. Yes, yes, in earnest, so I perceive. I may naturally be dull of apprehension, but my feelings are quick enough. I comprehend too well. Yes, it is impossible to judge of a woman before marriage, or to guess what sort of a wife she will make. I presume you speak from experience. You have been disappointed yourself and repent your choice.

Mr. B. My dear, what did I say that was like this? Upon my word, I meant no such thing. I really was not thinking of you in the least.

Mrs. B. No, you never think of me now. I can easily believe that you were not thinking of me in the least.

Mr. B. But I said that, only to prove to you that I could not be thinking ill of you, my dear.

Mrs. B. But I would rather that you thought ill of me, than that you did not think of me at all.

Mr. B. Well, my dear, I will even think ill of you, if that will please you.

Mrs. B. Do you laugh at me? When it comes to this, I am wretched indeed. Never man laughed at the woman he loved. As long as you had the slightest remains of love for me, you could not make me an object of derision: ridicule and love are incompatible, absolutely incompatible. Well, I have done my best, my very best, to make you happy, but in vain. I see I am not *cut out* to be a good wife. Happy, happy Mrs. Granby!

Mr. B. Happy, I hope sincerely, that she will be with my friend, but my happiness must depend on you, my love. So, for my sake, if not for your own, be composed and do not torment yourself with such fancies.

Mrs. B. I do wonder whether this Mrs. Granby

is really that Miss Emma Cooke. I'll go and see her directly. See her I must.

Mr. B.   I am heartily glad of it, my dear, for I am sure a visit to his wife will give my friend Granby real pleasure.

Mrs. B.   I promise you, my dear, I do not go to give him pleasure, or you either, but to satisfy my own *curiosity*.

QUESTIONS — 1. Describe the personalities of Mr. and Mrs. Bolingbroke. 2. Do you think Mr. Bolingbroke was speaking with irony when he said, "Indeed, my love, that is a very just observation"? 3. How does Mrs. Bolingbroke interpret most of her husband's statements that follow the one quoted in Question 2?

SPELL AND DEFINE — newspaper, stale, paragraph, provoking, apprehension, experience, disappointed, incompatible, curiosity.

LESSON XXXVIII (38)

The Blind Preacher—WIRT

As I traveled through the county of Orange, my eye was caught by a cluster of horses tied near a ruinous, old, wooden house in the forest, not far from the roadside. Having frequently seen such objects before, in traveling through these states, I had no difficulty in understanding that this was a place of religious worship.

Devotion alone should have stopped me to join in the duties of the congregation, but I must confess, that curiosity to hear the preacher of such a wilderness, was not the least of my motives. On entering I was struck with his unusual appearance. He was a tall and very spare old man; his head, which was covered with a white linen cap, his shriveled hands, and his voice, were all shaking under the influence of a palsy; and a few moments ascertained to me that he was perfectly blind.

The first emotions that touched my breast were those of mingled pity and veneration. But how soon were all my feelings changed? The lips of Plato were never more worthy of a prognostic swarm of bees, than were the lips of this holy man! It was a day of the administration of the sacraments, and his subject was, of course, the passion of our Savior. I had heard the subject handled a thousand times. I had thought it exhausted long ago. Little did I suppose, that in the wild woods of America I was to meet with a man, whose eloquence would give to this topic a new and more sublime pathos, than I had ever before witnessed.

As he descended from the pulpit to distribute the mystic symbols, there was a peculiar, a more than human solemnity in his air and manners, which made my blood run cold and my whole frame shiver. He then drew a picture of the sufferings of our Savior: his trial before Pilate, his ascent up Calvary, his crucifixion. I knew the whole history, but never until then had I heard the circumstances so selected, so arranged, so colored. It was all new, and I seemed to have heard it for the first time in my life. His enunciation was so deliberate that his voice trembled on every syllable. Every heart in the assembly trembled in unison.

His peculiar phrases had that force of description, that the original scene appeared to be at that moment acting before our eyes. We saw the very faces of the Jews: the staring, frightful distortions of malice and rage. We saw the buffet. My soul kindled with a flame of indignation, and my hands were involuntarily and convulsively clinched.

But when he came to touch on the patience, the forgiving meekness of our Savior; when he drew, to the life, his voice breathing to God a soft and gentle prayer of pardon on his enemies, "Father, forgive them, for they know not what they do," the voice of the preacher, which had all along faltered, grew fainter, until his utterance being entirely obstructed by the force of his feelings, he raised his handkerchief to his eyes and burst into a loud and irrepressible flood of grief. The effect was inconceivable. The whole house resounded with the mingled groans and sobs and shrieks of the congregation.

It was some time before the tumult had subsided, so far as to permit him to proceed. Indeed, judging by the usual, but fallacious standard of my own weakness, I began to be very uneasy for the situation of the preacher. For I could not conceive how he would be able to let his audience down from the height to which he had wound them, without impairing the solemnity and dignity of the subject, or perhaps shocking them by the abruptness of his fall. But, no: the descent was as beautiful and sublime, as the elevation had been rapid and enthusiastic.

The first sentence, with which he broke the awful silence, was a quotation from Rousseau: "Socrates died like a philosopher, but Jesus Christ, like a God!" I despair of giving you any idea of the effect produced by this short sentence, unless you could perfectly conceive the whole manner of the man, as well as the peculiar crisis in the discourse. Never before did I completely understand what Demosthenes meant by laying such stress on delivery.

You are to bring before you the venerable figure of the preacher; his blindness, constantly recalling to your recollection old Homer, Ossian, and Milton, and associating with his performance the melancholy grandeur of their geniuses; you are to imagine that you hear his slow, solemn, well-accented enunciation, and his voice of affecting, trembling melody; you are to remember the pitch of passion and enthusiasm to which the congregation were raised; and then, the few moments of portentous, death-like silence, which reigned throughout the house; the preacher, removing his white handkerchief from his aged face, (even yet wet from the recent torrent of his tears), and slowly stretching forth the palsied hand which held it, begins the sentence, "Socrates died like a philosopher"—then, pausing, raising his other, pressing them both, clasped together, with warmth and energy, to his breast, lifting his sightless eyes to heaven, and pouring his whole soul into his tremulous voice— "but Jesus Christ—like a God!"

This man has been before my imagination almost ever since. A thousand times as I rode along, I dropped the reins of my bridle, stretched forth my hand, and tried to imitate his quotation from Rousseau; a thousand times I abandoned the attempt in despair, and felt persuaded that his peculiar manner and power arose from an energy of soul, which nature could give, but which no human being could justly copy. As I recall, at this moment, several of his awfully striking attitudes, the chilling tide with which my blood begins to pour along my arteries, reminds me of the emotions produced by the first sight of Gray's introductory picture of his Bard.*

*_The Bard_ is a grandiloquent ode written by the English poet Thomas Gray.

QUESTIONS — 1. Describe the personal appearance of the blind preacher. 2. What was the topic of his sermon? 3. When he described the character and conduct of the Savior, what was the effect on the congregation? 4. What was the secret of the preacher's great power?

SPELL AND DEFINE — (2) palsy; (4) crucifixion; (5) description, convulsively; (6) utterance; (7) impairing, solemnity; (8) perfectly, delivery; (9) grandeur, enunciation; (10) energy, introductory.

LESSON XXXIX (39)

Apostrophe to Light—MILTON

NOTE—In this opening to Book III of *Paradise Lost*, the blind Milton addresses Light with a prayer to grant him inward light "that I may see and tell / Of things invisible to mortal sight."

1. Hail! holy Light, offspring of Heaven first born,
   Or of the eternal, coeternal beam,
   May I express thee unblamed? Since God is light,
   And never but in unapproached light
5. Dwelt from eternity, dwelt then in thee,
   Bright effluence of bright essence increate.
   Or hear'st thou, rather, pure ethereal stream,
   Whose fountain who shall tell? Before the sun,
   Before the heavens thou wert, and at the voice
10. Of God, as with a mantle, didst invest
   The rising world of waters dark and deep,
   Won from the void and formless infinite.

   Thee I revisit now with bolder wing,
   Escaped the Stygian pool, though long detained
15. In that obscure sojourn, while in my flight,
   Through utter and through middle darkness borne
   With other notes than to the Orphean lyre,
   I sung of chaos and eternal night,
   Taught by the heavenly muse to venture down
20. The dark descent, and up to reascend,

Though hard and rare. Thee I revisit safe,
And feel thy sovereign, vital lamp; but thou
Revisit'st not these eyes that roll in vain,
To find thy piercing ray, and find no dawn;
25. So thick a drop-serene hath quenched their orbs,
Or dim suffusion vailed. Yet not the more
Cease I to wander where the muses haunt,
Clear spring, or shady grove, or sunny hill,
Smit with the love of sacred song; but chief
30. Thee, Sion, and the flowery brooks beneath,
That wash thy hallowed feet, and warbling flow,
Nightly I visit; nor sometimes forget
Those other two, equaled with me in fate,
So were I equaled with them in renown,
35. Blind Thamyris* and blind Maeonides,†
And Tiresias and Phineus, prophets old:
Then feed on thoughts that voluntary move
Harmonious numbers, as the wakeful bird
Sings darkling, and in shadiest covert hid,
40. Tunes her nocturnal note. Thus with the year,
Seasons return, but not to me returns
Day, or the sweet approach of even and morn;
Or sight of vernal bloom, or summer's rose;
Or flocks, or herds, or human face divine;
45. But cloud, instead and ever-during dark
Surrounds me, from the cheerful ways of men
Cut off, and for the book of knowledge fair
Presented with a universal blank
Of nature's works, to me expunged and razed,
50. And wisdom, at one entrance, quite shut out.
So much the rather thou, celestial Light,
Shine inward, and the mind through all her powers
Irradiate: there plant eyes, all mist from thence
Purge and disperse, that I may see and tell
55. Of things invisible to mortal sight.

*A celebrated musician of Thrace, who was blind.   †A name of Homer.

QUESTIONS — 1. In poetical terms an apostrophe is a figure of speech in which someone or something is directly addressed as though present. In addressing Light, how does Milton characterize it? 2. It is said that Milton composed in his mind portions of his epic *Paradise Lost* each night after he retired and then in the morning dictated them. Read lines 26–32 and explain how these lines relate part of that procedure. 3. What does Milton say his blindness denies him? 4. What is his request to Light? (See lines 51–55)

SPELL AND DEFINE — (7) ethereal; (12) void; (15) obscure; (22) vital;   (27) haunt;   (34) renown;   (39) covert;   (43) vernal; (51) celestial; (54) disperse; (55) invisible.

LESSON XL (40)

View from Mt. Etna
LONDON ENCYCLOPEDIA

NOTE—Mt. Etna, on the island of Sicily, is the highest active volcano in Europe. Its height and crater are subject to constant change; its base covers approximately 500 square miles. The name Etna comes from a Greek word meaning "I burn."

The man who treads Mount Etna seems like a man above the world. When the sun arises, the prospect from the summit of Etna is beyond comparison the finest in nature. The eye rolls over it with astonishment and is lost. The diversity of objects, the extent of the horizon, the immense height, the country like a map at our feet, the ocean around, the heavens above—all conspire to overwhelm the mind and affect it.

We must be allowed to extract Mr. Brydone's description of this scene. "There is not," he says, "on the surface of the globe any one point that unites so many awful and sublime objects. The immense elevation from the surface of the earth, drawn as it were to a single point, without any neighboring mountain for the senses and imagination to rest upon and recover from their astonishment, in their way down to the world.

"This point or pinnacle, raised on the brink of a bottomless gulf, as old as the world, often discharges rivers of fire and throws out burning rocks with a noise that shakes the whole island. Add to this the unbounded extent of the prospect, comprehending the greatest diversity and the most beautiful scenery in nature, with the rising sun advancing in the east to illuminate the wondrous scene.

"The whole atmosphere by degrees kindles up, and shows dimly and faintly the boundless prospect around. Both sea and land appear dark and confused, as if only emerging from their original chaos, and light and darkness seem still undivided; till the morning, by degrees advancing, completes the separation. The stars are extinguished, and the shades disappear.

"The forests, which but just now seemed black and bottomless gulfs, from whence no ray was reflected to show their form or colors, appear a new creation rising to sight, catching life and beauty from every increasing beam. The scene still enlarges, and the horizon seems to widen and expand itself on all sides, until the sun, like the great Creator, appears in the east and with his plastic ray completes the mighty scene.

"All appears enchantment. And it is with difficulty we can believe we are still on earth. The senses, unaccustomed to the sublimity of such a scene, are bewildered and confounded; and it is not until after some time, that they are capable of separating and judging of the objects that compose it.

"The body of the sun is seen rising from the ocean, immense tracts both of sea and land intervening; the islands of Lipari, Panari, Alicudi, Strombolo, and Volcano, with their smoking summits, appear under your feet. You look down on the whole of Sicily as on a map and can trace every river through all its windings from its source to its mouth.

"The view is absolutely boundless on every side; nor is there any one object within the circle of vision to interrupt it, so that the sight is everywhere lost in the immensity. And I am persuaded, it is only from the imperfection of our eyes, that the coasts of Africa and even of Greece are not discovered, as they are certainly above the horizon. The circumference of the visible horizon on the top of Etna cannot be less than two thousand miles.

"The most beautiful part of the scene is certainly the mountain itself, the island of Sicily, and the numerous islands lying round it. All these, by a kind of magic in vision, that I am at a loss to account for, seem as if they were brought close round the skirts of Etna, the distances appearing reduced to nothing.

"Perhaps this singular effect is produced by the rays of light passing from a rarer medium into a denser, which, (from a well-known law in optics,) to an observer in the rare medium, appears to lift up objects that are at the bottom of the dense one, as a piece of money placed in a basin appears lifted up as soon as the basin is filled with water.

"The Regione Deserta, of the frigid zone of Etna, is the first object that calls your attention. It is marked out by a circle of snow and ice, which extends on all sides to the distance of about eight miles. In the center of this circle, the great crater of the mountain rears its burning head, and the regions of intense cold, and of intense heat, seem forever to be united in the same point.

"The Regione Deserta is immediately succeeded by the Sylvosa, or the woody region, which forms a circle or girdle of the most beautiful green, which surrounds the mountain on all sides, and is certainly one of the most delightful spots on earth."

QUESTIONS — 1. How does the rising sun enhance the view from the summit? 2. Name the different sights visible from the summit. 3. If you were at the top of the mountain, what different regions or kinds of country would you pass through before you would reach the bottom? 4. How active is the volcanic Mt. Etna? (Check an encyclopedia or other reference book.)

SPELL AND DEFINE — (2) diversity, horizon, conspire; (3) sublime, astonishment; (4) pinnacle, comprehending, wondrous; (5) atmosphere, emerging, chaos, extinguished; (6) plastic; (7) unaccustomed, sublimity, bewildered; (8) intervening; (9) circumference; (11) basin.

LESSON XLI (41)

The Alps—W. GAYLORD CLARK

Proud monuments of God! sublime ye stand
Among the wonders of His mighty hand:
With summits soaring in the upper sky,
Where the broad day looks down with burning eye;
Where gorgeous clouds in solemn pomp repose,
Flinging rich shadows on eternal snows:
Piles of triumphant dust, ye stand alone,
And hold, in kingly state, a peerless throne!

Like olden conquerors, on high ye rear
The regal ensign, and the glittering spear:
Round icy spires the mists, in wreaths unrolled,
Float ever near, in purple or in gold:
And voiceful torrents, sternly rolling there,
Fill with wild music the unpillared air:
What garden, or what hall on earth beneath,
Thrills to such tones, as o'er the mountains breathe?

There, though long ages past, those summits shone
When morning radiance on their state was thrown;
There, when the summer day's career was done,
Played the last glory of the sinking sun;
There, sprinkling luster o'er the cataract's shade,
The chastened moon her glittering rainbow made;
And blent with pictured stars, her luster lay,
Where to still vales the free streams leaped away.

Where are the thronging hosts of other days,
Whose banners floated o'er the Alpine ways;
Who, through their high defiles, to battle, wound,
While deadly ordnance stirred the heights around?
Gone; like the dream that melts at early morn,
When the lark's anthem through the sky is borne:
Gone; like the wrecks that sink in ocean's spray,
And chill Oblivion murmurs, Where are they?

Yet "Alps on Alps" still rise; the lofty home
Of storms and eagles, where their pinions roam;
Still roam their peaks and magic colors lie,
Of morn and eve, imprinted on the sky;
And still, while kings and thrones shall fade and fall,
And empty crowns lie dim upon the pall;
Still shall their glaciers flash, their torrents roar,
Till kingdoms fail, and nations rise no more.

QUESTIONS — 1. To whom are the Alps compared? 2. What
question is asked in stanza 4? What answer is given? 3. In what

way are the Alps superior to kings and thrones? 4. What is the rhyme scheme used in this poem?

SPELL AND DEFINE — (1) monuments, gorgeous, triumphant, peerless; (2) olden, ensign, voiceful, unpillared; (3) luster, cataract; (4) ordnance, oblivion, murmur; (5) glaciers.

LESSON XLII (42)

Respect for the Sabbath Rewarded
EDINBURGH PAPER

NOTE—Although it contains some incredible coincidences, this story, which is set in Bath, England, is supposedly based on fact. It fits well into the McGuffey formula of earthly as well as heavenly reward for the righteous. (Lindberg, p. 272.)

In the city of Bath, not many years ago, lived a barber, who made a practice of following his ordinary occupation on the Lord's day. As he was pursuing his morning's employment, he happened to enter into some place of worship just as the minister was giving out his text, "Remember the Sabbath day, to keep it holy." He listened long enough to be convinced that he was constantly breaking the laws of God and man by shaving and dressing his customers on the Lord's day. He became uneasy and went with a heavy heart to his Sabbath task.

At length he took courage and opened his mind to his minister, who advised him to give up Sabbath dressing, and worship God. He replied that beggary would be the consequence. He had a flourishing trade, but it would almost all be lost. At length, after many a sleepless night spent in weeping and praying, he was determined to cast all his care upon

God, as the more he reflected, the more his duty became apparent.

He discontinued Sabbath dressing, went constantly and early to the public services of religion, and soon enjoyed that satisfaction of mind which is one of the rewards of doing our duty, and that peace of God which the world can neither give nor take away. The consequences he foresaw, actually followed. His genteel customers left him, and he was nicknamed a Puritan or Methodist. He was obliged to give up his fashionable shop, and in the course of years became so reduced, as to take a cellar under the old market house and shave the common people.

One Saturday evening, between light and dark, a stranger from one of the coaches, asking for a barber, was directed by the hostler, to the cellar opposite. Coming in hastily, he requested to be shaved quickly, while they changed horses, *as he did not like to violate the Sabbath.* This was touching the barber on a tender chord. He burst into tears, asked the stranger to lend him a half-penny to buy a candle, as it was not light enough to shave him with safety. The man did so, considering in his mind the extreme poverty to which the poor man must be reduced.

While being shaved, he said, "There must be something extraordinary in your experience which I have not now time to hear. Here is half a crown for you. When I return, I will call and investigate your case. What is your name?"

"William Reed," said the astonished barber.

"William Reed?" echoed the stranger. "William Reed? By your dialect you are from the West."

"Yes, sir, from Kingston, near Taunton."

"William Reed, from Kingston, near Taunton? What was your father's name?"

"Thomas."

"Had he any brother?"

"Yes, sir, one after whom I was named. But he went to the Indies, and, as we never heard from him, we supposed him to be dead."

"Come along, follow me," said the stranger, "I am going to see a person who says *his* name is William Reed of Kingston, near Taunton. Come and confront him. If you prove to be indeed he who you say you are, I have glorious news for you. Your uncle is dead and has left an immense fortune, which I will put you in possession of, when all legal doubts are removed."

They went by the coach, saw the pretended William Reed, and proved him to be an imposter. The stranger, who was a pious attorney, was soon legally satisfied of the barber's identity and told him that he had advertised for him in vain. Providence had now thrown him in his way, in a most extraordinary manner, and he had great pleasure in transferring a great many thousand pounds to a worthy man, the rightful heir of the property. Thus was man's extremity, God's opportunity. Had the poor barber possessed one *half-penny*, or even had credit for a *candle*, he might have remained unknown for years, but he trusted God, who never said, "Seek ye my face in vain."

QUESTIONS — 1. What brought to the barber's attention the subject of keeping the Sabbath? 2. How was the barber's business affected by his Sabbath keeping? 3. What circumstances led to his learning that he was heir to a large property? 4. Is a person always materially rewarded for obeying God?

SPELL AND DEFINE — (1) practice, occupation; (2) beggary, consequence; (4) hostler; (5) dialect; (6) confront, legal; (7) pretended, imposter, advertised, transferring.

LESSON XLIII (43)

Satan and Death at the Gate of Hell
MILTON

NOTE—No other poem contains such treasures of learning as *Paradise Lost*, from which this selection is taken. In this scene from Book II, the meeting of Satan with Sin and Death is a triumph in the creation of a sense of horror and revulsion. Milton based his imaginative personification on James 1:15.

1.   Meanwhile the adversary of God and man,
Satan, with thoughts inflamed of highest design,
Puts on swift wings,
      and towards the gates of hell
Explores his solitary flight! sometimes
5. He scours the right hand coast,
      sometimes the left,
Now shaves with level wing the deep, then soars
Up to the fiery concave towering high.
As when far off at sea a fleet descried
Hangs in the clouds, by equinoctial winds
10. Close sailing from Bengala, or the isles
Of Ternate and Tidore, whence merchants bring
Their spicy drugs; they, on the trading flood,
Through the wide Ethiopian to the cape,
Ply stemming nightly toward the pole: so seemed
15. Far off the flying fiend. At last appear
Hell's bounds, high reaching to the horrid roof,
And thrice three-fold the gates:
      three folds were brass,
Three iron, three of adamantine rock
Impenetrable, impaled with circling fire,
20. Yet unconsumed. Before the gates there sat
On either side a formidable shape;
The one seemed woman to the waist, and fair,

But ended foul in many a scaly fold
Voluminous and vast, a serpent armed
25. With mortal sting; about her middle round
A cry of hell-hounds, never ceasing, barked
With wide Cerberean mouths full loud, and rung
A hideous peal. Far less abhorred than these
Vexed Scylla, bathing in the sea that parts
30. Calabria from the hoarse Trinacrian shore:
Nor uglier follow the night-hag, when, called
In secret, riding through the air she comes,
Lured with the smell of infant blood, to dance
With Lapland witches, while the laboring moon
35. Eclipses at their charms. The other shape,
If shape it might be called that shape had none
Distinguishable in member, joint, or limb;
Or substance might be called
    that shadow seemed;
For each seemed either; black it stood as night,
40. Fierce as ten furies, terrible as hell,
And shook a dreadful dart; what seemed his head
The likeness of a kingly crown had on.
Satan was now at hand; and from his seat
The monster moving, onward came as fast
45. With horrid strides; hell trembled as he strode.
The undaunted fiend what this might be admired,
Admired, not feared; God and his Son except,
Created thing nought valued he, nor shunned.
And with disdainful look thus first began.
50.   "Whence, and what art thou, execrable shape!
That darest, though grim and terrible, advance
Thy miscreated front across my way
To yonder gates? Through them I mean to pass,
That be assured, without leave asked of thee:
55. Retire or taste thy folly; and learn by proof,
Hell-born! not to contend with spirits of heaven!"
    To whom the goblin, full of wrath, replied,
"Art thou that traitor angel, art thou he,

Who first broke peace in heaven,
      and faith, till then
60. Unbroken, and in proud rebellious arms
Drew after him the third part of heaven's sons
Conjured against the highest, for which both thou
And they, outcast from God, are here condemned
To waste eternal days in woe and pain?
65. And reckonest thou thyself
      with spirits of heaven,
Hell-doomed! and breathest defiance
      here and scorn,
Where I reign king, and, to inflame thee more,
Thy king and lord! Back to thy punishment,
False fugitive! and to thy speed add wings,
70. Lest with a whip of scorpions I pursue
Thy lingering, or with one stroke of this dart
Strange horror seize thee,
      and pangs unfelt before."
So spake the grisly terror, and in shape,
So speaking and so threatening, grew ten-fold
75. More dreadful and deformed: on the other side,
Incensed with indignation, Satan stood
Unterrified, and like a comet burned,
That fires the length of Ophiuchus huge
In the arctic sky, and from his horrid hair
80. Shakes pestilence and war. Each at the head
Leveled his deadly aim; their fatal hands
No second stroke intend; and such a frown
Each cast at the other, as when two black clouds
With heaven's artillery fraught, come rattling on
85. Over the Caspian, then stand front to front
Hovering a space, till winds the signal blow
To join their dark encounter in mid air:
So frowned the mighty combatants, that hell
Grew darker at their frown;
      so matched they stood;
90. For never but once more was either like

To meet so great a foe: and now great deeds
Had been achieved, whereof all hell had rung,
Had not the snaky sorceress, that sat
Fast by hell-gate, and kept the fatal key,
95. Risen, and with hideous outcry, rushed between.

QUESTIONS—Milton, the great Puritan poet and writer, made himself master of the Bible, the Talmud, the writings of the early Christian fathers and everything worth knowing in the literature of Rome, Greece, Italy, France, Spain, and England. His great learning finds expression in his poetry, and it takes intellectual effort on the part of the reader to decode and understand his masterpieces. However, the effort is rewarded. 1. Describe the gates of Hell, as Milton portrays them. (Lines 17–20) 2. Describe the shapes that are guarding Milton's Hell. Shape one (called a snaky sorceress in line 93 and elsewhere in the poem identified as Sin)—Lines 22–28. Shape two (called a goblin in line 57 and elsewhere in the poem identified as Death)—Lines 35–42. 3. When Satan is queried about his identification, what deeds are credited to a "traitor angel"? Lines 58–64. 4. Who claims to be king of Hell? Lines 66–68. 5. How does Satan react to threats? Lines 75–80. 6. Who prevented a great conflict between Satan and Death? Lines 93–95. 7. How did Milton use James 1:15 in this passage?

LESSON XLIV (44)

Evils of Dismemberment—WEBSTER

NOTE—"Examples of [Daniel] Webster's oratorical splendor were often selected for inclusion within the McGuffeys, and many of the passages dealt specifically with the subject of this speech—preserving the Union. . . . Webster's wish never to see the 'States dissevered, discordant, belligerent,' was granted, for he died before the outbreak of the Civil War." (Lindberg, pp. 347, 348.)

Gentlemen, the political prosperity which this country has attained, and which it now enjoys, it has acquired mainly through the instrumentality of the present government. While this agent continues, the capacity of attaining to still higher degrees of prosperity exists also.

We have, while this lasts, a political life, capable of beneficial exertion, with power to resist or overcome misfortunes, to sustain us against the ordinary accidents of human affairs, and to promote by active efforts every public interest.

But dismemberment strikes at the very being which preserves these faculties. It would lay its rude and ruthless hand on this great agent itself. It would sweep away, not only what we possess, but all power of regaining lost or acquiring new possessions.

It would leave the country, not only bereft of its prosperity and happiness, but without limbs and organs or faculties by which to exert itself, hereafter, in the pursuit of that prosperity and happiness.

Other misfortunes may be borne or their effects overcome. If disastrous war should sweep our commerce from the ocean, another generation may renew it; if it exhaust our treasury, future industry may replenish it; if it desolate and lay waste our fields, still, under a new cultivation, they will grow green again, and ripen to future harvests.

It were but a trifle, even if the walls of yonder capitol were to crumble, if its lofty pillars should fall, and its gorgeous decorations be all covered by the dust of the valley. All these might be rebuilt. But who shall re-construct the fabric of demolished government? Who shall rear again the well-proportioned columns of constitutional liberty! Who shall frame together the skillful architecture which unites national sovereignty with state-rights, individual security, and public prosperity?

No, gentlemen, if these columns fall, they will be raised not again. Like the Coliseum and the Parthenon, they will be destined to a mournful, a melancholy immortality. Bitterer tears, however, will flow over them, than were ever shed over the monuments of Roman or Grecian art, for they will be the remnants of a more glorious edifice than Greece or Rome ever saw—the edifice of constitutional American liberty.

But, gentlemen, let us hope for better things. Let us trust in that gracious Being who has hitherto held our country as in the hollow of his hand. Let us trust to the virtue and the intelligence of the people and to the efficacy of religious obligation. Let us trust to the influence of Washington's example.

Let us hope that that fear of heaven, which expels all other fear, and that regard to duty, which transcends all other regard, may influence public men and private citizens, and lead our country still onward in her happy career. Full of these gratifying anticipations and hopes, let us look forward to the end of that century which is now commenced.

And may the disciples of Washington then see, as

we now see, the flag of the Union floating on the top of the capitol. And then, as now, may the sun in his course visit no land more free, more happy, more lovely, than this our own country!

QUESTIONS — 1. How was the political prosperity of this country obtained, according to Webster? 2. What does Webster consider to be the functions of government? 3. Why does Webster consider dismemberment (the break up of the Union) such a tragedy? 4. The capitol building could be reconstructed, but what could not be reconstructed? (Note the series of rhetorical questions.)

SPELL AND DEFINE — (1) instrumentality, government; (2) beneficial, misfortunes; (3) dismemberment, ruthless; (5) disastrous, replenish; (6) gorgeous, decorations, demolished, well-proportioned, constitutional, architecture, sovereignty; (7) melancholy; (9) transcends, anticipation.

LESSON XLV (45)

No Excellence Without Labor—WIRT

NOTE—This selection, written by a U.S. Attorney General, has appeared in every edition of the READERS. Its message was "stressed in many of the McGuffey lessons, but stated here so forcefully that this short piece became a standard entry in declamation contests for the rest of the [19th] century." (Lindberg, p. 226.)

The education—moral and intellectual—of every individual must be chiefly his own work. Rely upon it, that the ancients were right: both in morals and intellect, we give final shape to our characters and thus become, emphatically, the architects of our own fortune. How else could it happen that young men, who have had precisely the same opportunities, should be continually presenting us with such different results, and rushing to such opposite destinies?

Difference of talent will not solve it, because that difference is very often in favor of the disappointed candidate. You will see issuing from the walls of the same college, nay, sometimes from the bosom of the same family, two young men, of whom one will be admitted to be a genius of high order, the other scarcely above the point of mediocrity; yet you will see the genius sinking and perishing in poverty, obscurity, and wretchedness; while, on the other hand, you will observe the mediocre plodding his slow but sure way up the hill of life, gaining steadfast footing at every step and mounting at length to eminence and distinction, an ornament to his family, a blessing to his country.

Now, whose work is this? Manifestly their own. They are the architects of their respective fortunes. The best seminary of learning that can open its portals to you, can do no more than to afford you the opportunity of instruction: but it must depend, at last, on yourselves, whether you will be instructed or not, or to what point you will push your instruction.

And of this be assured, I speak from observation a certain truth: THERE IS NO EXCELLENCE WITHOUT GREAT LABOR. It is the fiat of fate, from which no power of genius can absolve you.

Genius, unexerted, is like the poor moth that flutters around a candle till it scorches itself to death. If genius be desirable at all, it is only of that great and magnanimous kind, which, like the condor of South America, pitches from the summit of Chimborazo, above the clouds, and sustains itself at pleasure in that empyreal region with an energy rather invigorated than weakened by the effort.

It is this capacity for high and long-continued exertion, this vigorous power of profound and searching investigation, this careering and wide-spreading comprehension of mind, and these long reaches of thought, that

"Pluck bright honor from the pale-faced moon,
 Or dive into the bottom of the deep,
 And drag up drowned honor by the locks;"

this is the prowess, and these the hardy achievements, which are to enroll your names among the great men of the earth.

QUESTIONS — 1. Whose responsibility is your education, according to Wirt? 2. What metaphor did the ancients use to express this principle? 3. What do the high achievements of one son and the low achievements of another son from the same family prove to the writer? 4. Why doesn't Wirt believe that achievement is based on intelligence? 5. How do the moth and the condor—one negatively and one positively—illustrate Wirt's thesis that "there is no excellence without great labor"?

SPELL AND DEFINE — (1) education, intellectual, emphatically, precisely; (2) obscurity, eminence, distinction; (3) manifestly, opportunity; (5) magnanimous, invigorated; (6) investigation, comprehension.

LESSON XLVI (46)

Christ and the Blind Man—BIBLE

NOTE—The Jews generally believed that all suffering was the result of wrongdoing. In the dramatic story of this miracle, Jesus confronts the issue and heals a man born blind. The ensuing conflict with the Pharisees leads the blind man to worship Jesus as Lord, and the Pharisees, ironically, to ask, "Are we blind also?"

John 9

1. And as Jesus passed by, he saw a man which was blind from his birth. And his disciples asked him, saying, Master, who did sin, this man or his parents, that he was born blind? Jesus answered, Neither hath this man sinned nor his parents, but that the works of God should be made manifest in him. I must work the works of him that sent me, while it is day; the night cometh when no man can work. As long as I am in the world, I am the light of the world.

2. When he had thus spoken, he spat on the ground, and made clay of the spittle, and he anointed the eyes of the blind man with the clay, and said unto him, Go, wash in the pool of Siloam, (which is, by interpretation, Sent). He went his way, therefore, and washed, and came seeing.

3. The neighbors therefore, and they which before had seen him that he was blind, said, Is not this he that sat and begged? Some said, This is he; others said, He is like him; but he said, I am he. Therefore said they unto him, How were thine eyes opened? He answered and said, A man that is called Jesus, made clay, and anointed mine eyes, and said unto me, Go to the pool of Siloam, and wash: and I

went and washed, and I received sight. Then said they unto him, Where is he? He said, I know not.

4. They brought to the Pharisees him that afore time was blind. And it was the Sabbath day when Jesus made the clay, and opened his eyes. Then again the Pharisees also asked him how he had received his sight. He said unto them, He put clay upon mine eyes, and I washed and do see. Therefore said some of the Pharisees, This man is not of God, because he keepeth not the Sabbath day. Others said, How can a man that is a sinner, do such miracles? And there was a division among them.

5. They say unto the blind man again, What sayest thou of him, that he hath opened thine eyes? He said, He is a prophet. But the Jews did not believe concerning him that he had been blind, and received his sight. And they asked them, saying, Is this your son, who ye say was born blind? How then doth he now see? His parents answered them and said, we know that this is our son, and that he was born blind: but by what means he now seeth, we know not: or who hath opened his eyes, we know not: he is of age, ask him, he shall speak for himself.

6. These words spake his parents, because they feared the Jews. for the Jews had agreed already, that if any man did confess that he was Christ, he should be put out of the synagogue. Therefore said his parents, He is of age, ask him.

7. Then again called they the man that was blind, and said, Give God the praise; we know that this man is a sinner. He answered and said, Whether he be a sinner or no, I know not; one thing I know, that, whereas I was blind, now I see. Then said they to him again, What did he to thee? How opened he thine eyes? He answered them, I have told you already, and ye did not hear: wherefore would ye hear it again? Will ye also be his disciples?

8. Then they reviled him, and said, Thou art his disciple; but we are Moses' disciples. We know that God spake unto Moses: as for this fellow, we know not from whence he is. The man answered and said unto them, Why, herein is a marvelous thing, that ye know not from whence he is, and yet he hath opened mine eyes. Now we know that God heareth not sinners: but if any man be a worshiper of God, and doeth his will, him he heareth. Since the world began, was it not heard, that any man opened the eyes of one that was born blind. If this man were not of God, he could do nothing. They answered, and said unto him, Thou wast altogether born in sins, and dost thou teach us? And they cast him out.

9. Jesus heard that they had cast him out; and when he had found him, he said unto him, Dost thou believe on the Son of God? He answered and said, Who is he, Lord, that I might believe on him? And Jesus said unto him, Thou hast both seen him, and it is he that talketh with thee. And he said, Lord, I believe. And he worshiped him.

10. And Jesus said, For judgment I am come into this world: that they which see not, might see; and that they which see, might be made blind. And some of the Pharisees which were with him heard these words, and said unto him, Are we blind also? Jesus said unto them, If ye were blind, ye should have no sin; but now ye say, We see; therefore your sin remaineth.

QUESTIONS — 1. What philosophical question did the disciples raise concerning the blind man? Why? 2. What two theological questions were raised by the miracle, causing a division among the Pharisees? 3. During the questioning by the Pharisees, whom did the former blind man say he believed Jesus to be? 4. After the former blind man was cast out of the synagogue, Jesus found him and led him to make what confession?

SPELL AND DEFINE — (2) interpretation; (3) neighbors; (4) Pharisees, miracles; (5) concerning; (6) confess; (7) sinner; (8) worshiper, altogether; (10) judgment.

LESSON XLVII (47)

Control Your Temper—TODD

NOTE—Roger Sherman, who began his career as a shoemaker and farmer, became an American political leader of the Revolutionary era and signer of the Declaration of Independence. Under the new Constitution he served in Congress, first as a representative and then as a senator. His qualities of character made Sherman a symbol of patriotic dedication and puritan simplicity to his own and later generations.

No one has a temper naturally so good that it does not need attention and cultivation; and no one has a temper so bad, but that by proper culture, it may become pleasant. One of the best disciplined tempers ever seen was that of a gentleman who was naturally quick, irritable, rash, and violent; but, by having the care of the sick, and especially of deranged people, he so completely mastered himself, that he was never known to be thrown off his guard.

The difference in the happiness which is received or bestowed by the man who governs his temper, and that by the man who does not, is immense. There is no misery so constant, so distressing, and so intolerable to others, as that of having a disposition which is your master and which is continually fretting itself. There are corners enough at every turn in life, against which we may run, and at which we may break out in impatience, if we choose.

Look at Roger Sherman, who rose from a humble occupation to a seat in the first Congress of the

United States, and whose judgment was received with great deference by that body of distinguished men. He made himself master of his temper and cultivated it as a great business in life. There are one or two instances which show this part of his character in a light that is beautiful.

One day, after having received his highest honors, he was sitting and reading in his parlor. A roguish student, in a room close by, held a mirror in such a position, as to pour the reflected rays of the sun directly in Mr. Sherman's face. He moved his chair, and the thing was repeated. A *third* time the chair was moved, but the mirror still reflected the sun in his eyes. He laid aside his book, went to the window, and many witnesses of the impudence expected to hear the ungentlemanly student severely reprimanded. He raised the window gently, and then—shut the window-blind!

I cannot forbear adducing another instance of the power he had acquired over himself. He was naturally possessed of strong passions, but over these he at length obtained an extraordinary control. He became habitually calm, sedate, and self-possessed. Mr. Sherman was one of those men who are not ashamed to maintain the forms of religion in their families. One morning he called them all together, as usual, to lead them in prayer to God. The "old family Bible" was brought out and laid on the table.

Mr. Sherman took his seat and placed beside him one of his children, a child of his old age. The rest of the family were seated around the room; several of these were now grown up. Besides these, some of the tutors of the college were boarders in the family and were present at the time alluded to. His aged and senile mother occupied a corner of the room, opposite the place where the distinguished Judge sat.

At length, he opened the Bible and began to read. The child who was seated beside him made some little disturbance, upon which Mr. Sherman paused and told it to be still. Again he proceeded, but again he paused to reprimand the little offender, whose playful disposition would scarcely permit to be still. At this time, he gently tapped its ear. The blow, if blow it might be called, caught the attention of his aged mother, who with some effort, rose from the seat and tottered across the room. At length, she reached the chair of Mr. Sherman, and in a moment, most unexpectedly to him, she gave him a blow on the ear with all the force she could summon. "There," said she, "you strike *your* child, and I will strike *mine.*"

For a moment, the blood was seen mounting to the face of Mr. Sherman, but it was *only* for a moment; then all was calm and mild as usual. He paused; he raised his spectacles; he cast his eye upon his mother; again it fell upon the book from which he had been reading. Not a word escaped him, but again he calmly pursued the service and soon after, sought in prayer an ability to set an example before his household, which should be worthy of their imitation. Such a victory was worth more than the proudest one ever achieved on the field of battle.

QUESTIONS — 1. According to the author, how often does life provide us with occasion to lose our temper? 2. How did witnesses expect Mr. Sherman to react to the student who was annoying him? What did he do? 3. What caused Mr. Sherman's mother to react so violently to her son's discipline of his own small child? 4. How does the author rate victory over one's temper?

SPELL AND DEFINE — (1) deranged; (2) intolerable, impatience; (3) cultivated; (4) impudence; (5) adducing, acquired, sedate; (6) senile, distinguished; (7) summon; (8) ability, imitation, example.

LESSON XLVIII (48)

Henry Martyn and Lord Byron
MISS BEECHER

NOTE—Henry Martyn (1781–1812) was an English missionary to India. He translated the New Testament into Urdu and into Persian, and the Psalms into Persian. While on a journey across Asia Minor, he was compelled by prostration to stop at Tokat, although the plague was raging there. He fell victim to the plague and died in a short time. Lord George Byron (1788–1824) was a widely read English romantic poet and, for a time, the darling of London society. His flamboyant and immoral personal life caused his name—during his own lifetime—to become a byword for dissoluteness.

Obedience to the law of God is the true path to happiness. To exhibit this, perhaps a fairer illustration cannot be presented than the contrasted records of two youthful personages who have made the most distinguished figure in the Christian, and the literary worlds: Henry Martyn, the missionary, and Lord Byron, the poet.

Martyn was richly endowed with ardent feelings, keen susceptibilities, and superior intellect. He was the object of many affections, and in the principal University of Great Britain, won the highest honors, both in classic literature and mathematical science. He was flattered and admired; the road to fame and honor lay open before him, and the brightest hopes of youth seemed ready to be realized.

But the hour came when he looked upon a lost and guilty world, in the light of eternity; when he realized the full meaning of the sacrifice of our incarnate God; when he assumed his obligations to become a fellow worker in recovering a guilty world from the dominion of sin and all its future woes.

"The love of God constrained him"; and without a murmur, for wretched beings on a distant shore, whom he never saw, of whom he knew nothing but that they were miserable and guilty, he relinquished the wreath of fame, forsook the path of worldly honor, severed the ties of kindred, and gave up friends, country, and home. With every nerve throbbing in anguish at the sacrifice, he went forth alone, to degraded heathen society, to solitude and privation, to weariness and painfulness, and to all the trials of missionary life.

He spent his days in teaching the guilty and degraded the way of pardon and peace. He lived to write the law of his God in the language of the Persian nation and to place a copy in the hands of its king. He lived to contend with the chief Moullahs of Mohammed in the mosques of Shiras and to kindle a flame in Persia, more undying than its fabled fires.

He lived to endure rebuke and scorn, to toil and suffer in a fervid clime, to drag his weary steps over burning sands, with the daily dying hope, that at last he might be laid to rest among his kindred and on his native shore. Yet even this last earthly hope was not attained, for after spending all his youth in ceaseless labors for the good of others, at the early age of thirty-two, he was laid in an unknown and foreign grave.

He died *alone*, a stranger in a strange land, with no friendly form around to sympathize with and soothe him. Yet this was the last record of his dying hand: "I sat in the orchard, and thought with sweet comfort and peace of my God! in solitude, my company! my friend! my comforter!"

And in reviewing the record of his short, yet blessed life, even if we forget the exulting joy with which such a benevolent spirit must welcome to heaven the thousands he toiled to save; if we look only at his years of self-denying trial, where were accumulated all the sufferings he was ever to feel, we can find *more* evidence of *true happiness*, than is to be found in the records of the youthful poet, who was gifted with every susceptibility of happiness, who spent his days in search of selfish enjoyment, who had every source of earthly bliss laid open, and drank to the very dregs.

We shall find that a mind which obeys the law of God is happier when bereft of the chief joys of this world, than a worldly man can be when possessed of them all. The remains of Lord Byron present one of the most mournful exhibitions of a noble mind in all the wide chaos of ruin and disorder. He, also, was naturally endowed with overflowing affections, keen sensibilities, quick conceptions, and a sense of moral rectitude. He had all the constituents of a mind of first-rate order. But he passed through existence amid the wildest disorder of a ruined spirit.

His mind seemed utterly unbalanced, teeming with rich thoughts and overbearing impulses, the sport of the strangest fancies and the strongest passions; bound down by no habit, restrained by no principle; a singular combination of great conceptions and fantastic caprices, of manly dignity and childish folly, of noble feeling and babyish weakness.

The Lord of Newstead Abbey, the heir of a boasted line of ancestry, a peer of the realm, the pride of the social circle, the leading star of poesy, the hero of Greece, the wonder of the gaping world, can now be followed to his secret haunts. And there the veriest child of the nursery might be amused at some of his silly weaknesses and ridiculous conceits. Distressed about the cut of a collar, fuming at the color of his dress, intensely anxious about the whiteness of his hands, deeply engrossed with monkeys and dogs, he flew about from one whim to another, with a reckless earnestness as ludicrous as it is disgusting.

At times, this boasted hero and genius, seemed naught but an overgrown child that had broken its leading strings and overmastered its nurses. At other times, he is beheld in all the rounds of dissipation and the haunts of vice, occasionally filling up his leisure in recording and disseminating the disgusting minutia of his weakness and shame, and with an effrontery and stupidity equaled only by that of the friend who retails them to the insulted world.

Again we behold him philosophizing like a sage and moralizing like a Christian, while often from his bosom burst forth the repinings of a wounded spirit. He sometimes seemed to gaze upon his own mind with wonder, to watch its disordered powers with curious inquiry, to touch its complaining strings and start at the response; while often with maddening sweep he shook every chord and sent forth its deep wailings to entrance a wondering world.

Both Henry Martyn and Lord Byron shared the sorrows of life, and their records teach the different workings of the Christian and the worldly mind. Byron lost his mother, and when urged not to give way to sorrow, he burst into an agony of grief, saying, "I had but *one* friend in the world, and now she is gone!" On the death of some of his early friends, he thus writes: "My friends fall around me, and I shall be left a lonely tree before I am withered. *I have no resource but my own reflections* and they present no prospect here or hereafter, except the selfish satisfaction of surviving my betters. I am indeed most wretched."

And thus Henry Martyn mourns the loss of one most dear: "Can it be that she has been lying so many months in the cold grave? Would that I could always remember it, or always forget it; but to think a moment on other things, and then feel the remembrance of it come, as if for the first time, rends my heart asunder. O my gracious God, what should I do without Thee! But now thou art manifesting thyself as 'the God of all consolation.' Never was I so near thee. There is nothing in the world for which I could wish to live, except because it may please God to appoint me some work to do. O thou incomprehensibly glorious Savior, what hast thou done to alleviate the sorrows of life!"

At anniversaries, when the mind is called to review life and its labors, they recorded their thoughts. Thus Byron writes: "At twelve o'clock I shall have completed thirty-three years! I go to my bed with a heaviness of heart at having lived so long and to so little purpose. It is now three minutes past twelve, and I am thirty-three!

'Alas, my friend, the years pass swiftly by.'

But I do not regret them so much for what I have done, as for what I *might* have done."

And thus Martyn: "I like to find myself employed usefully, in a way I did not expect or foresee. The coming year is to be a perilous one, but my life is of little consequence, whether I finish the Persian New Testament or not. I look back with pity on myself, when I attached so much importance to my life and labors. The more I see of my own works, the more I am ashamed of them, for coarseness and clumsiness mar all the works of man. I am sick when I look at the wisdom of man, but am relieved by reflecting, that we have a city whose builder and maker is God. The least of *his* works is refreshing. A dried leaf or a straw makes me feel *in good company*, and complacency and admiration take the place of disgust. What a momentary duration is the life of man! 'It glides along, rolling onward forever,' may be affirmed of the river; but men pass away as soon as they begin to exist. Well, let the moments pass!

> 'They waft us sooner o'er
>   This life's tempestuous sea,
> Soon we shall reach the blissful shore
>   Of blest eternity!' "

Such was the experience of those who in youth completed their course. The poet has well described his own career:

> "A wandering mass of shapeless flame,
> A pathless comet and a curse,
> The menace of the universe;
> Still rolling on with innate force,
> Without a sphere, without a course,
> A bright deformity on high,
> The monster of the upper sky!"

In holy writ we read of those who are "raging waves of the sea, foaming out their own shame; *wandering stars*, to whom is reserved the blackness of darkness forever." The lips of man may not apply these terrific words to any whose doom is yet to be disclosed; but there is a passage which none can fear to apply. "Those that are wise, shall shine as the brightness of the firmament; and they that turn many to righteousness, as stars forever and forever!"

QUESTIONS — 1. Compare the talents of Martyn and Byron. 2. Why did Martyn give up the prospects of fame and fortune to live a life of hardship and obscurity as a missionary? 3. What demonstrates Byron's weakness of character? 4. How did Martyn and Byron each feel about the value of his own life?

SPELL AND DEFINE — (1) personages; (3) dominion; (7) sympathizes; (8) exulting; (9) exhibitions, constituents; (10) impulses; (11) ancestry, engrossed; (12) haunts, disseminating; (13) sage; (17) perilous, clumsiness, duration.

LESSON XLIX (49)

Henry First After Death of His Son
MRS. FELICIA HEMANS

NOTE—"Henry I, king of England, who commenced his reign A.D. 1100, had a son called William, a brave and noble-minded youth, who had arrived at his eighteenth year. The king loved him most tenderly, and took care to have him recognized as his successor by the states of England and carried him over to Normandy, in the north of France, to receive the homage of the barons of that duchy. On the prince's return, the vessel in which he embarked was wrecked. He was placed in a boat and might have escaped, had he not been called back by the cries of his sister. He prevailed on the sailors to row back and take her in. But no sooner had the boat approached the wreck, than numbers who had been left, jumped into it, and the whole were drowned. King Henry, when he heard of the death of his son, fainted away, and from that moment, *he never smiled again.*" (From McGuffey's FOURTH READER, 1853 ed., pp. 42, 43.)

> The bark that held the prince went down,
>   The sweeping waves rolled on;—
> And what was England's glorious crown
>   To him that wept a son?
> He lived—for life may long be borne,
>   Ere sorrow breaks its chain;
> Still comes not death to those who mourn;
>   He never smiled again!
>
> There stood proud forms before his throne,
>   The stately and the brave;

But which could fill the place of one,
   That one beneath the wave?
Before him passed the young and fair,
   In pleasure's reckless train?
But seas dashed o'er his son's bright hair—
   He never smiled again!

He sat where festal bowls went round;
   He heard the minstrel sing;
He saw the tourney's victor crowned
   Amid the mighty ring;—
A murmur of the restless deep
   Mingled with every strain,
A voice of winds that would not sleep:—
   He never smiled again!

Hearts in that time, closed o'er the trace
   Of vows once fondly poured;
And strangers took the kinsman's place
   At many a joyous board;
Graves, which true love had bathed with tears,
   Were left to heaven's bright rain;
Fresh hopes were born for other years:—
   He never smiled again!

QUESTIONS — 1. How did Henry I's son die? At what age?
2. What things failed to console the king? 3. Each stanza ends
with the line, "He never smiled again." Do you think this state-
ment is literally true? Or, in what other sense might it be true?

SPELL AND DEFINE — (1) bark; (2) reckless; (3) festal, tourney; (4) vows, kinsman, joyous.

LESSON L (50)

Effects of Gambling—TIMOTHY FLINT

NOTE—Movies and television often portray the Western gambler of frontier days as a romantic and heroic figure. In this selection an eye-witness to the frontier gamblers destroys this image, and in its place reveals the results of indulging in this vice.

The love of gambling steals, perhaps, more often than any other sin, with an imperceptible influence on its victim. Its first pretext is inconsiderable, and falsely termed innocent play, with no more than the gentle excitement necessary to amusement. This plea, once indulged, is but too often "as the letting out of water." The interest imperceptibly grows. Pride of superior skill, opportunity, avarice, and all the overwhelming passions of depraved nature, ally themselves with the incipient and growing fondness. Dam and dike are swept away. The victim struggles in vain and is borne down by the uncontrolled current.

Thousands have given scope to the latent guilty avarice, unconscious of the guest they harbored in their bosoms. Thousands have exulted over the avails of gambling, without comprehending the baseness of using the money of another, won without honest industry, obtained without an equivalent—and perhaps from the simplicity, rashness, and inexperience of youth. Multitudes have commenced gambling, thinking only to win a small sum and prove their superior skill and dexterity, and there pause.

But it is the teaching of all time, it is the experience of human nature, that effectual resistance to powerful propensities, if made at all, is usually made before the commission of the first sin. My dear reader, let me implore you, by the mercies of God and the worth of your soul, to contemplate this enormous evil only from a distance. Stand firmly against the first temptation, under whatsoever specious forms it may assail you. "Touch not." "Handle not." "Enter not into temptation."

It is the melancholy and well known character of this sin, that, where once an appetite for it has gained possession of the breast, the common motives, the gentle excitements, and the ordinary inducements to business or amusement are no longer felt. It incorporates itself with the whole body of thought and fills with its fascination all the desires of the heart. Nothing can henceforward arouse the spell-bound victim to a pleasurable consciousness of existence, but the destructive stimulus of gambling.

Another appalling view of gambling is, that it is *the prolific stem, the fruitful parent, of all other vices.* Blasphemy, falsehood, cheating, drunkenness, quarreling, and murder, are all naturally connected with gambling. What has been said, with so much power and truth, of another sin, may, with equal emphasis and truth, be asserted of this: "Allow yourself to become a confirmed gambler; and detestable as this practice is, it will soon be only one among many gross sins of which you will be guilty." Giving yourself up to the indulgence of another sinful course, might prove your ruin, but then you might perish only under the guilt of the indulgence of a single gross sin.

But should you become a gambler, you will, in all probability, descend to destruction with the added infamy of having been the slave of all kinds of ini-

quity, and "led captive by Satan at his will."
Gambling seizes hold of all the passions, allies itself
with all the appetites, and compels every propensity
to pay tribute. The subject, however plausible in his
external deportment, becomes avaricious, greedy,
insatiable. Meditations upon the card table occupy
all his day and night dreams. Had he the power, he
would annihilate all the hours of this our short life,
that necessarily intervene between the periods of
his favorite pursuit.

Cheating is a sure and inseparable attendant
upon a continued course of gambling. We well know
with what horror the canons of the card table repel
this charge. It pains us to assert our deep and
deliberate conviction of its truth. There must be
prostration of moral principle, and silence of conscience, even to begin with it. Surely a man who
regards the natural sense of right, laying the obligations of Christianity out of the question, cannot sit
down with the purpose to win the money of another
in this way.

He must be aware in doing it, that avarice and
dishonest thoughts—it may be almost unconsciously to himself—mingle with his motives. Having once
closed his eyes upon the unworthiness of his
motives and deceived himself, he begins to study
how he may deceive others. Every moralist has re-
marked upon the delicacy of conscience; and that,
from the first violation, it becomes more and more
callous, until finally it sleeps a sleep as of death and
ceases to remonstrate. The gambler is less and less
scrupulous about the modes of winning, so that he
can win. No person will be long near the gambling
table of high stakes, be the standing of the players
what it may, without hearing the charge of CHEAT-
ING bandied back and forward, or reading the in-
dignant expression of it in their countenances. One

half of our fatal duels have their immediate or remote origin in insinuations of this sort.

The alternations of loss and gain; the abnormal excitement of the mind, and consequent depression when that excitement has passed away; the bacchanalian merriment of guilty associates; the loss of natural rest; in short, the very atmosphere of the gambling table, foster the temperament of *hard drinking*. A keen sense of interest may, indeed, and often does, restrain the gambler, while actually engaged in his employment, that he may possess the requisite coolness to watch his antagonist and avail himself of every passing advantage.

But the moment the high excitement of play is intermitted, the moment the passions vibrate back to the state of repose, what shall sustain the sinking spirits; what shall renerve the relaxed physical nature; what shall fortify the mind against the tortures of conscience, and the thoughts of "a judgment to come," but intoxication? It is the experience of all time, that a person is seldom a gambler for any considerable period, without being also a drunkard.

Blasphemy follows, as a thing of course: and is, indeed, the well-known and universal dialect of the gambler. How often has my heart sunk within me, as I have passed the dark and dire receptacles of the gambler, and seen the red and bloated faces, and inhaled the mingled smells of tobacco and potent drink; and heard the loud, strange, and horrid curses of the players; realizing the while, that these beings so occupied were candidates for eternity, and now on the course which, if not speedily forsaken, would fix them forever in hell.

We have already said, that gambling naturally leads to *quarreling and murder*. How often have we retired to our berth in the steamboat and heard charges of dishonesty, accents of reviling and re-crimination, and hints that these charges must be met and settled at another time and place, ring in our ears as we have been attempting to commune with God and settle in a right frame to repose! Many corpses of young men, who met a violent death from this cause, have we seen carried to their long home! Every gambler, in the region where we write, is always armed to the teeth and goes to his horrid pursuit as the gladiator formerly presented himself on the arena of combat.

The picture receives deeper shades, if we take into the grouping the *wife*, or the *daughter* or the *mother*, who lies sleepless and ruminating through the long night, trembling lest her midnight retirement shall be invaded by those who bring back the husband and the father wounded or slain, in one of those sudden frays which the card table, its accompaniments, and the passions it excites, so frequently generate. Suppose these forebodings should not be realized, and that he should steal home alive in the morning, with beggary and drunkenness, guilt and despair, written on his haggard countenance and accents of sullenness and ill temper falling from his tongue. How insupportably gloomy must be the prospects of the future to that family!

These are but feeble and general sketches of the misery and ruin to individuals and to society from the indulgence of this vice, during the present life. If the wishes of unbelief were true, and there were no life after this, what perverse and miserable calculations would be those of the gambler, taking into view only the present world! But, in any view of the character and consequences of gambling, who shall dare close his eyes upon its *future bearing* on the interest and the eternal welfare of his soul! Who shall dare lay out of the calculation the *retributions of eternity?*

Say thou, my youthful reader, I implore thee, looking up to the Lord for a firm and unalterable purpose, "I will hold fast my integrity and not let it go!"

QUESTIONS — 1. How does the interest in gambling develop? 2. To what other vices does gambling lead? 3. Who suffer because of a person's gambling? 4. What is the only sure way not to become ensnared in the trap of gambling? 5. In the cities that today permit gambling casinos, is there any evidence of a higher-than-average crime rate, compared with other cities of similar size?

SPELL AND DEFINE — (2) latent; (3) effectual, contemplate, specious; (4) melancholy; (5) prolific, indulgence; (6) intervene; (7) inseparable; (8) unconsciously; (9) antagonist; (10) vibrate; (11) inhaled, potent; (13) ruminating, forebodings, haggard; (14) calculations.

LESSON LI (51)

The Miser—POLLOK

NOTE—This poem was included in the first edition of the FOURTH READER, which was published a decade before the California Gold Rush began. But after 1849, students and teachers must have read a timely message into the poem.

1. Gold many hunted, sweat and bled for gold;
   Waked all the night, and labored all the day;
   And what was this allurement, dost thou ask?
   A dust dug from the bowels of the earth,
5. Which, being cast into the fire, came out
   A shining thing that fools admired, and called
   A god; and in devout and humble plight

Before it kneeled, the greater to the less;
And on its altar, sacrificed ease, and peace,
10. Truth, faith, integrity, good conscience, friends,
Love, charity, benevolence, and all
The sweet and tender sympathies of life;
And, to complete the horrid, murderous rite,
And signalize their folly, offered up
15. Their souls, and an eternity of bliss,
To gain them; what? an hour of dreaming joy,
A feverish hour that hasted to be done,
And ended in the bitterness of woe.
Most, for the luxuries it bought, the pomp,
20. The praise, the glitter, fashion, and renown,
This yellow phantom followed and adored.
But there was one in folly, further gone,
With eye awry, incurable, and wild,
The laughingstock of devils and of men,
25. And by his guardian angel quite given up,
The *miser*, who with dust inanimate
Held wedded loyalties.
       Ill-guided wretch!
Thou might'st have seen him
       at the midnight hour,
30. When good men slept, and in light-winged dreams
Ascended up to God,—in wasteful hall,
With vigilance and fasting, worn to skin
And bone, and wrapped in most debasing rags,
Thou might'st have seen him bending
       o'er his heaps,
35. And holding strange communion with his gold;
And as his thievish fancy seemed to hear
The night-man's foot approach, starting alarmed,
And in his old, decrepit, withered hand,
That palsy shook, grasping the yellow earth,
40. To make it sure.
       Of all god made upright,
And in their nostrils breathed a living soul,

Most fallen, most prone, most earthy,
  most debased;
Of all that sold Eternity for Time,
45. None bargained on so easy terms with death.
Illustrious fool! Nay, most inhuman wretch!
He sat among his bags, and, with a look
Which hell might be ashamed of, drove the poor
Away unalmsed, and mid abundance died,
50. Sorest of evils! died of *utter want.*

QUESTIONS — 1. What were men willing to endure in order to get gold? 2. What were they willing to sacrifice for gold? 3. What names does the poem use to refer to gold? 4. In what sense did the miser die of "utter want" amid "abundance"?

SPELL AND DEFINE—bowels, integrity, charity, sympathies, murderous, signalize, bitterness, luxuries, pomp, awry, incurable, guardian, inanimate, illustrious.

LESSON LII (52)

Death at the Vanity Table
DIARY OF A PHYSICIAN

NOTE—Death was certainly not a topic to be avoided in the McGuffey READERS. Usually, a religious purpose motivated the subject, pointing readers toward the rewards and punishments of a judgment to come.

"What can Charlotte be doing all this while?" inquired her mother. She listened—"I have not heard her moving for the last three quarters of an hour! I will call the maid and ask." She rang the bell, and the servant appeared.

"Betty, Miss Jones is not gone yet, is she? Go up to her room, Betty, and see if she wants anything, and tell her it is half past nine o'clock," said Mrs.

Jones. The servant accordingly went up stairs and knocked at the bedroom door, once, twice, thrice, but received no answer. There was a dead silence, except when the wind shook the window. Could Miss Jones have fallen asleep? Oh! impossible!

She knocked again, but as unsuccessfully as before. She became a little flustered, and after a moment's pause opened the door and entered. There was Miss Jones sitting at the glass. "Why ma'am!" commenced Betty in a petulant tone, walking up to her, "here have I been knocking for these five minutes, and"——Betty staggered, horror struck to the bed, and uttering a loud shriek, alarmed Mrs. Jones, who instantly tottered up stairs, almost palsied with fright. Miss Jones was dead!

I was there within a few minutes, for my house was not more than two streets distant. It was a stormy night in March: and the desolate aspect of things without—deserted streets—the dreary howling of the wind; and the incessant pattering of the rain—contributed to cast a gloom over my mind, when connected with the intelligence of the awful event that had summoned me out, which was deepened into horror by the spectacle I was doomed to witness.

On reaching the house, I found Mrs. Jones in violent hysterics, surrounded by several of her neighbors who had been called to her assistance. I repaired to the scene of death and beheld what I never shall forget.

The room was occupied by a white-curtained bed. There was but one window, and before it was a table on which stood a mirror hung with a little white drapery. Various paraphernalia lay scattered about—pins, brooches, curling papers, ribbons, gloves, etc.

An arm chair was drawn to this table, and in it

sat Miss Jones, stone dead. Her head rested upon her right hand, her elbow supported by the table; while her left hung down by her side, grasping a pair of curling irons. Each of her wrists was encircled by a showy gilt bracelet.

She was dressed in a white muslin frock, with a little bordering of blonde. Her face was turned towards the mirror, which by the light of the expiring candle reflected with frightful fidelity the clammy, fixed features, daubed with scarlet rouge—the fallen lower jaw—and the eyes directed full into the glass, with a cold stare that was appalling.

On examining the countenance more narrowly, I thought I detected the traces of a smirk of conceit and self-complacency, which not even the palsying touch of death could wholly obliterate. The hair of the corpse, all smooth and glossy, was curled with elaborate precision, and the skinny sallow neck was encircled with a string of glistening pearls. The ghastly visage of death thus leering through the tinselry of fashion—the "vain show" of artificial joy—was a horrible mockery of the fooleries of life!

Indeed it was a most humiliating and shocking spectacle. Poor creature! struck dead in the very act of sacrificing at the shrine of vanity!

On examination of the body, we found that death had been occasioned by disease of the heart. Her life might have been protracted, possibly for years, had she but taken my advice and that of her mother.

I have seen many hundreds of corpses, as well in the calm composure of natural death, as mangled and distorted by violence. But never have I seen so startling a satire upon human vanity, so repulsive, unsightly, and loathsome a spectacle, as a *corpse dressed for a ball!*

QUESTIONS — 1. What was the young woman Charlotte doing at the time of her death? 2. Who describes the death scene in this story? How did he compare it with others he had seen? 3. Why was this scene a "satire upon human vanity"?

SPELL AND DEFINE — (3) flustered, palsied; (4) desolate, spectacle; (5) hysterics; (6) paraphernalia, brooches; (7) gilt; (9) self-complacency, obliterate, sallow, visage; (11) protracted; (12) satire.

LESSON LIII (53)

The Patriotism of Western Literature
DR. DRAKE

NOTE—"The early editions of the McGuffey READERS were heavily promoted as the textbooks of the West, and this lesson serves as a good example of such regional pride—free from 'foreign influences.' " (Lindberg, p. 147.) The author, Dr. Daniel Drake, who was a prominent physician, educator, and civic leader in Cincinnati, selected William McGuffey to be President of the new Cincinnati College. (Lindberg, p. 148.)

Our literature cannot fail to be patriotic, and its patriotism will be American—composed of a love of country, mingled with an admiration for our political institutions.

To feel in his heart and infuse into his writings, the inspiration of such a patriotism, the scholar must feast his taste on the delicacies of our scenery and dwell with enthusiasm on the genius of our constitution and laws. Thus sanctified in its character, this sentiment becomes a principle of moral and intellectual dignity—an element of fire, purifying and subliming the mass in which it glows.

As a guiding star to the will, its light is inferior only to that of Christianity. Heroic in its philanthropy, untiring in its enterprises, and sublime in the martyrdoms it willingly suffers, it justly occupies a high place among the virtues which ennoble the human character. A literature, animated with this patriotism, is a national blessing, and such will be the literature of the West.

The literature of the whole Union must be richly endowed with this spirit, but a double portion will be the lot of the interior, because the foreign influences which dilute and weaken this virtue in the extremities, cannot reach the heart of the continent, where all that lives and moves is American.

Hence a native of the West may be confided in as his country's hope. Compare him with the native of a great maritime city on the verge of the nation,— his birthplace the fourth story of a house, hemmed in by surrounding edifices, his play-ground a pavement, the scene of his juvenile rambles an arcade of shops, his young eyes feasted on the flags of a hundred alien governments, the streets in which he wanders crowded with foreigners, and the ocean, common to all nations, forever expanding to his view.

Estimate *his* love of country, as far as it depends on local and early attachments, and then contrast him with the young backwoodsman, born and reared amidst objects, scenes, and events, which you can all bring to mind—the jutting rocks in the great road, half alive with organic remains or sparkling with crystals; the quiet old walnut tree, dropping its nuts upon the yellow leaves, as the morning sun melts the October frost; the grape-vine swing; the chase after the cowardly black snake, till it creeps under the rotten log; the sitting down to rest upon the crumbling trunk, and an idle examination of the mushrooms and mosses which grow from its ruins.

Then the wading in the shallow stream, and up-turning of the flat stones to find bait with which to fish in the deeper waters; next the plunder of a bird's nest, to make necklaces of the speckled eggs, for her who has plundered him of his young heart; then the beech tree with its smooth body, on which he cuts the initials of her name interlocked with his own; finally, the great hollow stump, by the path that leads up the valley to the log school-house, its dry bark peeled off, and the stately polk-weed grow-ing from its center, and bending with crimson ber-ries, which invite him to sit down and write upon its polished wood. How much pleasanter it is to extract ground squirrels from beneath its roots, than to ex-tract the square root, under that labor-saving machine, the ferule of a teacher!

The affections of one who is blest with such remi-niscences, like the branches of our beautiful trumpet flower, strike their roots into every sur-rounding object and derive support from all which stand within their reach. The love of country is with him a constitutional and governing principle. If he be a mechanic, the wood and iron which he molds into form, are dear to his heart because they remind him of his own hills and forests. If a husbandman, he holds companionship with growing corn, as the offspring of his native soil. If a legislator, his dreams are filled with sights of national prosperity to flow from his beneficent enactments. If a scholar devoted to the interests of literature, in his lone and excited hours of midnight study, while the winds are hushed and all animated nature sleeps, when the silence is so profound, that the stroke of his own pen grates, loud and harsh upon his ear, and fancy, from the great deep of his luminous intellect, draws up new forms of smiling beauty and solemn grandeur; the genius of his country hovers nigh, and sheds

over its pages an essence of patriotism, sweeter
than the honey-dew which the summer night distils
upon the leaves of our forest trees.

QUESTIONS — 1. How does an American develop patriotism?
2. Dr. Drake considers patriotism to be second in importance
only to what? 3. Describe the childhood of a child growing up in
a seaport city—according to Drake. 4. Describe the childhood of
a child growing up in the interior of the country—according to
Drake. 5. Do you believe that the average person in the interior
of this country is more patriotic than the average person living
on either coast? Why? Or why not?

SPELL AND DEFINE — (1) patriotism; (2. intellectual, sentiment; (3) philanthropy; (4) interior, extremities; (5) foreigners;
(6) attachments, crystals, cowardly; (7) ferule; (8) reminiscences,
constitutional, luminous.

LESSON LIV (54)

Christian Hymn of Triumph from
"The Martyr of Antioch"—MILMAN

Sing to the Lord! let harp, and lute, and voice,
Up to the expanding gates of heaven rejoice,
    While the bright martyrs to their rest are borne!
Sing to the Lord! their blood-stained course is run,
And every head its diadem hath won,
    Rich as the purple of the summer morn—
Sing the triumphant champions of their God,
While burn their mounting feet
        along their sky-ward road.

Sing to the Lord! for her, in beauty's prime,
Snatched from this wintry earth's ungenial clime,
    In the eternal spring of paradise to bloom;

For her the world displayed its brightest treasure,
And the airs panted with the songs of pleasure.
Before earth's throne she chose the lowly tomb,
The vale of tears with willing footsteps trod,
Bearing her cross with thee, incarnate Son of God.

Sing to the Lord! it is not shed in vain,
The blood of martyrs! from its freshening rain
  High springs the church like some
    fount-shadowing palm:
The nations crowd beneath its branching shade,
Of its green leaves are kingly diadems made,
  And, wrapt within its deep, embosoming calm,
Earth shrinks to slumber like the breezeless deep,
And war's tempestuous vultures fold their
    wings and sleep.

Sing to the Lord! no more the angels fly—
Far in the bosom of the stainless sky—
  The sound of fierce, licentious sacrifice.
From shrin'd alcove and stately pedestal,
The marble gods in cumbrous ruin fall;
  Headless, in dust, the awe of nations lies;
Jove's thunder crumbles in his mouldering hand,
And mute as sepulchers the hymnless temples stand.

QUESTIONS — 1. What were the two choices available to the young woman in stanza 2? Which did she choose? 2. Why isn't the martyrs' blood shed in vain?

SPELL AND DEFINE — (1) triumphant, champion; (2) ungenial, incarnate; (3) diadem, tempestuous, vultures; (4) licentious, alcove, cumbrous, sepulchers.

LESSON LV (55)

Comfort Ye My People—BIBLE

NOTE—In some of the most sublime language ever written, Isaiah, in chapters 40–66, looks forward to the time when Jerusalem's "warfare" will be over, when her Messiah will come and establish his kingdom. These chapters have earned for Isaiah the title of "gospel prophet." Handel drew heavily from the following chapter for his oratorio, *Messiah.*

Isaiah 40

Comfort ye, comfort ye my people!
Saith your God.
Speak ye comfortably to Jerusalem,
    and cry unto her,
That her warfare is accomplished,
5. That her iniquity is pardoned:
For she hath received of the Lord's hand
Double for all her sins.

The voice of him that crieth in the wilderness,
    Prepare ye the way of the Lord;
10.   Make straight in the desert a highway
        for our God!
    Every valley shall be exalted;
    And every mountain and hill shall
        be made low;
    And the crooked shall be made straight;
    And the rough places plain:
15.   And the glory of the Lord shall be revealed,
    And all flesh shall see it together:
    For the mouth of the Lord hath spoken it.
The voice said, Cry! And he said, What
        shall I cry?
    All flesh is grass,

20. And all the goodliness thereof is as the
             flower of the field:
         The grass withereth, the flower fadeth:
         Because the spirit of the Lord bloweth
             upon it:
         Surely the people is grass.
         The grass withereth, the flower fadeth:
25.   But the word of our God shall
             stand forever.
         O Zion, that bringest good tidings! get thee
             up into the high mountain;
         O Jerusalem, that bringest good tidings!
         Lift up thy voice with strength;
         Lift it up, be not afraid;
30.   Say unto the cities of Judah, Behold
             your God!
         Behold! the Lord your God will come with
             strong hand,
         And his arm shall rule for him:
         Behold! his reward is with him,
         And his work before him.
35.   He shall feed his flock like a shepherd:
         He shall gather the lambs with his arm,
         And carry them in his bosom,
         And shall gently lead those that are
             with young.
     Who hath measured the waters in the hollow
             of his hand,
40. And meted out heaven with the span,
     And comprehended the dust of the earth
             in a measure,
     And weighed the mountains in scales,
     And the hills in a balance?
     Who hath directed the spirit of the Lord,
45. Or, being his counselor, hath taught him?
     With whom took he counsel, and who
             instructed him,

And taught him in the path of judgment,
And taught him knowledge,
And showed to him the way of understanding?
50. Behold! the nations are as a drop of a bucket,
And are counted as the small dust
        of the balance:
Behold! he taketh up the isles as a
        very little thing.
And Lebanon is not sufficient to burn,
Nor the beasts thereof sufficient
        for a burnt offering.
55. All nations before him are as nothing;
And they are counted to him less than
        nothing, and vanity.
    To whom then will you liken Me,
Or shall I be equal? saith the Holy One.
Lift up your eyes on high, and behold!
60. Who hath created these things?
That bringeth out their host by number?
He calleth them all by names: by the
        greatness of his might,
            For that he is strong in power,
Not one faileth.
    Why sayest thou, O Jacob! and speakest,
        O Israel!
65. My way is hid from the Lord,
And my judgment is passed over
        from my God?
Hast thou not known? hast thou not heard,
That the everlasting God, the Lord,
The Creator of the ends of the earth,
70. Fainteth not, neither is weary?
There is no searching of his understanding.
He giveth power to the faint;
And to them that have no might he
        increaseth strength.
Even the youths shall faint and be weary,

75. And the young men shall utterly fall:
But they that wait upon the Lord shall renew
their strength;
They shall mount up with wings as eagles;
They shall run and not be weary;
And they shall walk, and not faint.

QUESTIONS — 1. Who applied the words of lines 8–10 to himself? (See John 1:19–23) 2. Why are lines 35–38 considered to be Messianic? (Compare John 10:11) 3. "To whom then will you liken Me, Or shall I be equal? saith the Holy One." What reason is given for the Holy One's being without equal? 4. What promise is given to those who "wait upon the Lord"?

SPELL AND DEFINE—comfortably, exalted, revealed, comprehended, counselor, faint, eagles.

LESSON LVI (56)

Value of Mathematics
E. D. MANSFIELD

NOTE—What? A student who does not like mathematics, but who wants to explore nature and learn the reason of things? This convincing essay declares that it is impossible for an inquiring person to escape mathematics. He may as well fly through space in search of another planet, for this earth "has no resting place for him."

Man may construct his works by irregular and uncertain rules, but God has made an unerring law for His whole creation, and made it, too, in respect to the physical system, upon principles, which, as far as we now know, can never be understood without the aid of mathematics.

Let us suppose a youth who despises, as many do, these *cold* and *passionless abstractions of the math-*

ematics. Yet, he is intellectual; he loves knowledge; he wants to explore nature, and know the reason of things; but he would do it without aid from this *rigid, syllogistic, measuring, calculating science.* He seeks indeed, no "royal road to geometry," but, he seeks one not less difficult to find, in which geometry is not needed.

He begins with the mechanical powers. He takes the lever and readily understands that it will move a weight. But the principle upon which *different* weights at *different* distances are moved, he is forbidden to know, for *they* depend upon *ratios* and *proportions.* He passes to the inclined plane, but quits it in disgust when he finds its action depends upon the relations of angles and triangles. When he comes to the wheel and axle, he gives them up forever; they are *all mathematical!*

He would investigate the laws of falling bodies, and moving fluids, and would know why their motion is *accelerated* at different periods, and upon what their momentum depends. But, roots and squares, lines, angles, and curves float before him in the mazy dance of a disturbed intellect. The very first proposition is a *mystery*, and he soon discovers that mechanical science is little better than mathematics itself.

But he still has his *senses*; he will, at least, not be indebted to diagrams and equations for their enjoyment. He gazes with admiration upon the phenomena of light; the many-colored rainbow upon the bosom of the clouds; the clouds themselves reflected with all their changing shades from the surface of the quiet waters. Whence comes this beautiful imagery? He investigates and finds that every hue in the rainbow is made by a different *angle of refraction*, and that each ray reflected from the mirror, has its angle of incidence equal to its angle of reflection. And, as he pursues the subject further, in the construction of lenses and telescopes, the whole family of triangles, ratios, proportions, and conclusions arise to alarm his excited vision.

He turns to the heavens and is charmed with its shining host, moving in solemn procession, "through the halls of the sky," each star, as it rises and sets, marking time on the records of nature. He would know the structure of this beautiful system, and search out, if possible, the laws which regulate those distant lights. But astronomy forever banishes him from her presence; she will have none near her to whom mathematics is not a *familiar friend*. What can *he* know of her parallaxes, anomalies, and precessions, who has never studied the conic sections, or the higher order of analysis? She sends him to some wooden orrery*, from which he may gather as much knowledge of the heavenly bodies, as a child does of armies from the gilded troopers of the toy shop.

But if he can have no companionship with optics, nor astronomy, nor mechanical science, there *are* sciences, he thinks, which have better taste and less austerity of manners. He flies to chemistry, and her garments float loosely around him. For a while, he goes gloriously on, illuminated by the *red lights* and *blue lights* of crucibles and retorts. But, soon he comes to compound bodies, to the composition of the elements around him, and finds them all in fixed relations. He finds that gases and fluids will combine with each other, and with solids only in a certain *ratio*, and that all possible compounds are formed by nature in *immutable proportion*. Then starts up the whole doctrine of chemical equivalents, and mathematics again stares him in the face.

Affrighted, he flies to mineralogy; stones he may pick up, jewels he may draw from the bosom of the earth and be no longer alarmed at the stern visage of this terrible science. But, even here, he is not safe. The first stone that he finds, quartz, contains a *crystal* and that crystal assumes the dreaded form of geometry. Crystallization allures him on, but, as he goes, cubes and hexagons, pyramids and dodecagons arise before him in beautiful array. He would understand more about them, but must *wait* at the portal of the temple, till introduced within by that honored of time and science, our friendly *Euclid.*

And now, where shall this student of nature, without the aid of mathematics, go for his knowledge, or his enjoyments? Is it to natural history? The very *birds* cleave the air in the form of the cycloid, and mathematics proves it the *best.* Their feathers are formed upon calculated mechanical principles; the muscles of their frame are moved by them. The little bee has constructed his cell in the very geometrical figure, and with the precise angles, which mathematicians, after ages of investigation, have demonstrated to be that which contains the greatest *economy of space and strength.* Yes! he, who would shun mathematics, must fly the bounds of "flaming space," and in the realms of chaos, that

"—— dark,
Illimitable ocean, ——"

where Milton's Satan wandered from the wrath of heaven, he may *possibly* find some spot visited by no figure of geometry and no harmony of proportion. But nature, this beautiful creation of God, has no resting place for him. All its construction is *mathematical;* all its uses, *reasonable;* all its ends, *harmonious.* It has no elements mixed without regulated law; no broken chord to make a false note in the music of the spheres.

*A clockwork model showing the motions of the planets around the sun. Invented in 1715 by George Graham at the expense of Charles Boyle, 4th Earl of Orrery.

QUESTIONS — 1. For what areas of study must a student have a knowledge of mathematics? 2. What areas of contemporary study, that were unknown to this writer, can you name as also dependent on mathematics? 3. Without mathematics, the writer argues, one's knowledge of nature will remain superficial. What colorful comparisons are given in paragraph six to illustrate this point?

SPELL AND DEFINE — (2) intellectual, explore, syllogistic, geometry; (3) mechanical, proportion, axle; (4) accelerated; (5) diagrams, equations, phenomena, refraction; (6) astronomy, orrery; (7) illuminate; (8) visage, portal, crystal; (9) cell, chaos, illimitable.

LESSON LVII (57)

Washing Day—MRS. BARBAULD

NOTE—Before the use of electrical power the "dreaded washing day" required a full day's labor by mother, maid, and older daughters. Water had to be drawn from a well or spring, carried to the kitchen stove or outdoor fire, heated, and poured into tubs. All by hand the clothes were washed, rinsed, starched, and hung on lines and fences or draped over shrubs to dry. In this delightful poem, the poet reminisces about her childhood impressions of washing day.

1. The Muses are turned gossips; they have lost
   The buskined step, and clear high-
        sounding phrase,
   Language of gods. Come then, domestic Muse,
   In slip-shod measure loosely prattling on
5. Of farm or orchard, pleasant curds and cream,
   Or drowning flies, or shoe lost in the mire
   By little whimpering boy, with rueful face;

Come, Muse, and sing the dreaded Washing Day.
Ye who beneath the yoke of wedlock bend,
10. With bowed soul, full well ye know the day
Which week, smooth sliding after week, brings on
Too soon; for to that day nor peace belongs
Nor comfort; ere the first gray streak of dawn,
The red-armed washers come and chase repose.
15. Nor pleasant smile, nor quaint device of mirth,
E'er visited that day: the very cat,
From the wet kitchen scared, and reeking hearth,
Visits the parlor, an unwonted guest.
The silent breakfast meal is soon dispatched,
20. Uninterrupted, save by anxious looks
Cast at the lowering sky, if sky should lower.
From that last evil, O preserve us, heavens!
For should the skies pour down, adieu to all
Remains of quiet: then expect to hear
25. Of sad disasters; dirt and gravel stains
Hard to efface, and loaded lines at once
Snapped short, and linen horse*
     by dog thrown down,
And all the petty miseries of life.
Saints have been calm while stretched
     upon the rack,
30. And Guatimozin smiled on burning coals;
But never yet did housewife notable
Greet with a smile a rainy washing day.
But grant the welkin fair, require not thou
Who call'st thyself perchance the master there,
35. Or study swept, or nicely dusted coat,
Or usual 'tendance; ask not, indiscreet,
Thy stockings mended, though the yawning rents
Gape wide as Erebus; nor hope to find
Some snug recess impervious: shouldst thou try
40. The 'customed garden walks, thine eye shall rue
The budding fragrance of thy tender shrubs,
Myrtle or rose, all crushed beneath the weight

Of coarse checked apron, with impatient hand
Twitched off when showers impend;
    or crossing lines
45. Shall mar thy musings, as the wet cold sheet
Flaps in thy face abrupt. Woe to the friend
Whose evil stars have urged him forth to claim,
On such a day, the hospitable rites!
Looks, blank at best, and stinted courtesy,
50. Shall he receive. Vainly he feeds his hopes
With dinner of roast chickens, savory pie,
Or tart or pudding: pudding he nor tart
That day shall eat: nor, though the husband try,
Mending what can't be helped, to kindle mirth
55. From cheer deficient, shall his consort's brow
Clear up propitious: the unlucky guest
In silence dines, and early slinks away.
I well remember, when a child, the awe
This day struck into me; for then the maids,
60. I scarce knew why, looked cross,
    and drove me from them;
Nor soft caress could I obtain, nor hope
Usual indulgences; jelly or creams,
Relic of costly suppers, and set by
For me, their petted one; or buttered toast,
65. When butter was forbid; or thrilling tale
Of ghost, or witch, or murder; so I went
And sheltered me beside the parlor fire:
There, my dear grandmother, eldest of forms,
Tended the little ones, and watched from harm,
70. Anxiously fond, though oft her spectacles
With elfin cunning hid, and oft the pins
Drawn from her raveled stockings,
    might have soured
One less indulgent.
At intervals my mother's voice was heard,
75. Urging dispatch: briskly the work went on,
All hands employed to wash, to rinse, to wring,

To fold, and starch, and clap, and iron, and plait.
Then would I sit me down and ponder much
Why washings were. Sometimes through
    hollow bowl
80. Of pipe amused we blew, and sent aloft
The floating bubbles; little dreaming then
To see, Mongolfier, thy silken ball
Ride buoyant through the clouds;
    so near approach
The sports of children and the toils of men.

---

*A long pole placed in the middle of a laundry line to keep it from sagging with the weight of the clothes.

QUESTIONS — 1. In the opening lines, the poetess warns us that instead of speaking in the language of the gods, for this poem the Muses will use the language of whom? 2. What was the general attitude of the household members on washing day? 3. What was always a threat to washing day—causing "sad disasters" and "all the petty miseries of life"? 4. How did washing day affect a visitor? the small children? someone who needed stockings mended? 5. What did the children do that makes the poetess philosophize, "So near approach/The sports of children and the toils of men"?

LESSON LVIII (58)

Capturing the Wild Horse—IRVING

NOTE—Indian half-breeds, rangers, and a Frenchman plot to capture wild horses in this adventure story from the frontier plains. Washington Irving's colorful description details all the fortunes and misfortunes that the hunt along the banks of the Red River presented.

We left the buffalo camp about eight o'clock, and had a toilsome and harassing march of two hours over ridges of hills covered with a ragged forest of scrub oaks and broken by deep gullies.

About ten o'clock in the morning, we came to where this line of rugged hills swept down into a valley through which flowed the north fork of Red River. A beautiful meadow, about half a mile wide, enameled with yellow autumnal flowers, stretched for two or three miles along the foot of the hills, bordered on the opposite side by the river, whose banks were fringed with cottonwood trees, the bright foliage of which refreshed and delighted the eye, after being wearied by the contemplation of monotonous wastes of brown forest.

The meadow was finely diversified by groves and clumps of trees, so happily disposed, that they seemed as if set out by the hand of art. As we cast our eyes over this fresh and delightful valley, we beheld a troop of wild horses, quietly grazing on a green lawn, about a mile distant to our right, while to our left at nearly the same distance, were several buffaloes; some feeding, others reposing, and ruminating among the high, rich herbage, under the shade of a clump of cottonwood trees. The whole had the appearance of a broad beautiful tract of pasture land on the highly-ornamented estate of some gentleman farmer, with his cattle grazing about the lawns and meadows.

A council of war was now held, and it was determined to profit by the present favorable opportunity and try our hand at the grand hunting maneuver, which is called "ringing the wild horse." This requires a large party of horsemen, well mounted. They extend themselves in each direction, at certain distances apart, and gradually form a ring of two or three miles in circumference, so as to surround the game. This must be done with extreme care, for the wild horse is the most readily alarmed inhabitant of the prairie and can scent a hunter at a great distance, if to windward.

The ring being formed, two or three ride toward the horses, which start off in an opposite direction. Whenever they approach the bounds of the ring, however, a huntsman presents himself and turns them from their course. In this way they are checked and driven back at every point and kept galloping round and round this magic circle, until, being completely tired down, it is easy for hunters to ride up beside them and throw the *lariat* over their heads. The prime horses of the most speed, courage, and bottom, however, are apt to break through and escape, so that, in general, it is the second-rate horses that are taken.

Preparations were now made for a hunt of this kind. The pack horses were now taken into the woods and firmly tied to trees, lest in a rush of wild horses, they should break away. Twenty-five men were then sent under the command of a lieutenant, to steal along the edge of the valley, within the strip of wood that skirted the hills. They were to station themselves about fifty yards apart, within the edge of the woods, and not advance or show themselves until the horses dashed in that direction. Twenty-five men were sent across the valley to steal in like manner along the river bank that bordered the opposite side and to station themselves among the trees.

A third party of about the same number was to form a line, stretching across the lower part of the valley, so as to connect the two wings. Beatte and our other half breed, Antoine, together with the officious Tonish, were to make a circuit through the woods, so as to get to the upper part of the valley, in the rear of the horses, and drive them forward into the kind of sack that we had formed, while the two wings should join behind them and make a complete circle.

The flanking parties were quietly extending themselves out of sight on each side of the valley, and the residue were stretching themselves like the links of a chain across it, when the wild horses gave signs that they scented an enemy; snuffing the air, snorting, and looking about. At length they pranced off slowly toward the river and disappeared behind a green bank.

Here, had the regulations of the chase been observed, they would have been quickly checked and turned back by the advance of a hunter from the trees; unluckily, however, we had our wild-fire, Jack-o'lantern, little Frenchman to deal with. Instead of keeping quietly up the right side of the valley, to get above the horses, the moment he saw them move toward the river, he broke out of the covert of woods and dashed furiously across the plain in pursuit of them. This put an end to all system. The half breeds and half a score of rangers joined in the chase.

Away they all went over the green bank. In a moment or two, the wild horses reappeared and came thundering down the valley, with Frenchman, half breeds, and rangers galloping and bellowing behind them. It was in vain that the line drawn across the valley, attempted to check and turn back the fugitives; they were too hotly pressed by their pursuers. In their panic they dashed through the line and clattered down the plain.

The whole troop joined in the headlong chase, some of the rangers without hats or caps, their hair flying about their ears, and others with handkerchiefs tied round their heads. The buffaloes, which had been calmly ruminating among the herbage, heaved up their huge forms, gazed for a moment at the tempest that came scouring down the meadow, then turned and took to heavy rolling flight. They were soon overtaken. The promiscuous throng were pressed together by the contracting sides of the valley, and away they went pell mell, hurry skurry, wild buffalo, wild horse, wild huntsman, with clang and clatter, and whoop and halloo, that made the forests ring.

At length, the buffaloes turned into a green brake on the river bank, while the horses dashed up a narrow defile of the hills, with their pursuers close at their heels. Beatte passed several of them, having fixed his eye upon a fine Pawnee horse that had his ears slit and saddle marks upon his back. He pressed him gallantly, but lost him in the woods.

Among the wild horses, was a fine black mare, which in scrambling up the defile, tripped and fell. A young ranger sprang from his horse, and seized her by the mane and muzzle. Another ranger dismounted and came to his assistance. The mare struggled fiercely, kicking and biting and striking with her fore feet, but a noose was slipped over her head and her struggles were in vain.

It was some time, however, before she gave over

rearing and plunging and lashing out with her feet on every side. The two rangers then led her along the valley, by two strong lariats, which enabled them to keep at a sufficient distance on each side, to be out of the reach of her hoofs, and whenever she struck out in one direction, she was jerked in the other. In this way her spirit was gradually subdued.

As to Tonish, who had marred the whole scheme by his precipitancy, he had been more successful than he deserved, having managed to catch a beautiful cream-colored colt about seven months old, that had not strength to keep up with its companions. The mercurial little Frenchman was beside himself with exultation. It was amusing to see him with his prize. The colt would rear and kick and struggle to get free, when Tonish would take him about the neck, wrestle with him, jump on his back, and cut as many antics as a monkey with a kitten.

Nothing surprised me more, however, than to witness how soon these poor animals thus taken from the unbounded freedom of the prairie, yielded to the dominion of man. In the course of two or three days, the mare and colt went with the lead horses, and became quite docile.

QUESTIONS — 1. Where did this hunt take place? Locate the general area on a map. 2. How did the group intend to capture the horses? 3. What caused these plans to be ineffective? 4. Give the striking contrast between the flight of the wild horses and that of the buffaloes. 5. What amazed Irving about the captured horses?

SPELL AND DEFINE — (1) buffalo; (2) autumnal, monotonous; (3) diversified; (5) magic, lariat; (6) skirted; (7) circuit; (8) pranced; (10) panic; (12) defile; (13) struggles; (14) subdued; (15) marred, scheme; (16) docile.

LESSON LIX (59)

The Best of Classics—GRIMKE

NOTE—Thomas Smith Grimke, who was a reformer for various causes, opposed the teaching of the classics (Greek and Roman literature) and argued for more instruction from the Bible. (Lindberg, p. 143.)

There is a classic, the best the world has ever seen, the noblest that has ever honored and dignified the language of mortals. If we look into its antiquity, we discover a title to our veneration, unrivaled in the history of literature. If we have respect to its evidences, they are found in the testimony of miracle and prophecy; in the ministry of man, of nature, and of angels, yea, even of "God, manifest in the flesh," of "God blessed forever."

If we consider its authenticity, no other pages have survived the lapse of time, that can be compared with it. If we examine its authority, for it speaks as never man spake, we discover that it came from heaven, in vision and prophecy under the sanction of Him, who is Creator of all things and the Giver of every good and perfect gift.

If we reflect on its truths, they are lovely and spotless, sublime and holy, as God himself, unchangeable as his nature, durable as his righteous dominion and versatile as the moral condition of mankind. If we regard the value of its treasures, we must estimate them, not like the relics of classic antiquity, by the perishable glory and beauty, virtue and happiness of this world, but by the enduring perfection and supreme felicity of an eternal kingdom.

If we inquire, who are the men that have recorded

its truths, vindicated its rights, and illustrated the excellence of its scheme, from the depth of ages and from the living world, from the populous continent and the isles of the sea, comes forth the answer: the patriarch and the prophet, the evangelist and the martyr.

If we look abroad through the world of men, the victims of folly or vice, the prey of cruelty, of injustice, and inquire what are its benefits, even in this temporal state, the great and the humble, the rich and the poor, the powerful and the weak, the learned and the ignorant reply, as with one voice, that humility and resignation, purity, order and peace, faith, hope, and charity, are its blessings upon earth.

And if, raising our eyes from time to eternity, from the world of mortals to the world of just men made perfect, from the visible creation, marvelous, beautiful, and glorious as it is, to the invisible creation of angels and seraphs, from the footstool of God, to the throne of God himself, we ask, what are the blessings that flow from this single volume, let the question be answered by the pen of the evangelist, the harp of the prophet, and the records of the book of life.

Such is the best of classics the world has ever admired; such, the noblest that man has ever adopted as a guide.

QUESTIONS — 1. What does the writer list as evidences for the truth of the Bible? 2. On what is the authority of the Bible based? 3. What blessings does the Bible bring to this earth?

SPELL AND DEFINE — (1) dignified, literature; (2) authenticity, examine; (3) dominion, estimate, felicity; (5) prey, temporal, resignation.

LESSON LX (60)

Egyptian Mummies and Tombs
BELZONI

NOTE—Giovanni Belzoni (1778–1823) was an Italian explorer of Egyptian antiquities. At Thebes he removed the colossal head of Ramses II for the British museum, and at Abu Simbel he cleared the great temple of Ramses II. Several archeological firsts are credited to him.

Gournou is a tract of rocks about two miles in length at the foot of the Lybian mountains on the west of Thebes, and was the burial place of the great city of a hundred gates. Every part of these rocks is cut out by art, in the form of large and of small chambers, each of which has its separate entrance; and though they are very close to each other, it is seldom that there is any interior communication from one to another. I can truly say, it is impossible to give any description sufficient to convey the smallest idea of those subterranean abodes and their inhabitants. There are no sepulchers in any part of the world like them; there are no excavations or mines that can be compared to these truly astonishing places; and no exact description can be given of their interior, owing to the difficulty of visiting these recesses. The inconvenience of entering into them is such, that it is not everyone who can support the exertion.

A traveler is generally satisfied when he has seen the large hall, the gallery, the staircase, and as far as he can conveniently go. Besides, he is so taken up with the strange works he observes cut in various places and painted on each side of the walls, that when he comes to a narrow and difficult passage or a descent to the bottom of a well or cavity, he declines taking such trouble, naturally supposing that he cannot see in these abysses anything so magnificent as what he sees above, and consequently deems it useless to proceed any farther.

Of some of these tombs many persons could not withstand the suffocating air, which often causes fainting. A vast quantity of dust rises, so fine that it enters into the throat and nostrils and chokes the nose and mouth to such a degree that it requires great power of lungs to resist it. And there is the strong smell of the mummies. This is not all: the entry or passage where the bodies are, is roughly cut in the rocks, and the falling of the sand from the upper part or ceiling of the passage causes it to be nearly filled up. In some places there is not more than a vacancy of a foot left, which you must contrive to pass through in a creeping posture like a snail, on pointed and keen stones, that cut like glass.

After getting through these passages, some of them two or three hundred yards long, you generally find a more commodious place, perhaps high enough to sit. But what a place of rest! surrounded by bodies, by heaps of mummies in all directions, which, previous to my being accustomed to the sight, impressed me with horror. The blackness of the wall, the faint light given by the candles or torches for want of air, the different objects that surrounded me, seeming to converse with each other, and the Arabs with the candles or torches in their hands, naked and covered with dust, themselves resembling living mummies, absolutely formed a scene that cannot be described. In such a situation I found myself several times, and often returned exhausted and fainting, till at last I became inured to it, and indifferent to what I suffered, except from the dust, which never failed to choke my throat and nose. And though, fortunately, I am destitute of the sense of smelling, I could taste that the mummies were rather unpleasant to swallow.

After the exertion of entering into such a place, through a passage of fifty, a hundred, three hundred, or perhaps six hundred yards, nearly overcome, I sought a resting-place, found one, and contrived to sit, but when my weight bore on the body of an Egyptian, it crushed like a bandbox. I naturally had recourse to my hands to sustain my weight, but they found no better support, so that I sank altogether among the broken mummies, with a crash of bones, rags, and wooden cases, which raised such a dust as kept me motionless for a quarter of an hour, waiting till it subsided again. I could not remove from the place, however, without increasing it, and every step I took I crushed a mummy in some part or other.

Once I was conducted from such a place to another resembling it, through a passage of about twenty feet in length and no wider than what a body could be forced through. It was choked with mummies, and I could not pass without putting my face in contact with that of some decayed Egyptian. As the passage inclined downwards, my own weight helped me on; however, I could not avoid being covered with bones, legs, arms, and heads, rolling from above. Thus I proceeded from one cave to another, all full of mummies piled up in various ways, some standing, some lying, and some on their heads.

The purpose of my researches was to rob the mummies of their papyri, of which I found a few hidden in their breasts under their arms, in the space above the knees, or on the legs, and covered by the

numerous folds of cloth that envelop the mummy.
The people of Gournou, who make a trade of antiquities of this sort, are very jealous of strangers and
keep them as secret as possible, deceiving travelers
by pretending that they have arrived at the end of
the pits, when they are scarcely at the entrance.

I must not omit, that among these tombs we saw
some which contained the mummies of animals intermixed with human bodies. There were bulls,
cows, sheep, monkeys, foxes, bats, crocodiles,
fishes, and birds in them. Idols often occur, and one
tomb was filled with nothing but cats, carefully
folded in red and white linen, the head covered by a
mask representing the cat and made of the same
linen. I have opened all these sorts of animals. Of
the bull, the calf, and the sheep, there is no part but
the head which is covered with linen, and the horns
project out of the cloth; the rest of the body being
represented by two pieces of wood, eighteen inches
wide and three feet long, in a horizontal direction, at
the end of which was another, placed perpendicularly, two feet high, to form the breast of the animal.

The calves and sheep are of the same structure,
and large in proportion to the bulls. The monkey is
in its full form, in a sitting posture. The fox is
squeezed up by the bandages, but in some measure
the shape of the head is kept perfect. The crocodile
is left in its own shape, and after being well bound
round with linen, the eyes and mouth are painted on
this covering. The birds are squeezed together, and
lose their shape, except the ibis, which is found like
a fowl ready to be cooked, and bound round with
linen like all the rest.

The next sort of mummy that drew my attention,
I believe I may with reason conclude to have been
appropriated to the priests. They are folded in a
manner totally different from the others, and so

carefully executed, as to show the great respect paid to those personages. The bandages are stripes of red and white linen intermixed, covering the whole body, and producing a curious effect from the two colors. The arms and legs are not enclosed in the same envelope with the body, as in the common mode, but are bandaged separately, even the fingers and toes being preserved distinct. They have sandals of painted leather on their feet and bracelets on their arms and wrists. They are always found with the arms across the breast, but not pressing it; and though the body is bound with such a quantity of linen, the shape of the person is carefully preserved in every limb. The cases in which mummies of this sort are found, are somewhat better executed, and I have seen one that had the eyes and eyebrows of enamel, beautifully executed in imitation of nature.

The dwelling place of the natives is generally in the passages, between the first and second entrance into a tomb. The walls and the roof are as black as any chimney. The inner door is closed up with mud, except a small aperture sufficient for a man to crawl through. Within this place the sheep are kept at night, and occasionally accompany their masters in their vocal concert. Over the doorway there are always some half-broken Egyptian figures, and the two foxes, the usual guardians of burial-places. A small lamp, kept alive by fat from the sheep or rancid oil is placed in a niche in the wall, and a mat is spread on the ground. This formed the grand divan wherever I was.

There the people assembled round me, their conversation turning wholly on antiquities. Such a one had found such a thing, and another had discovered a tomb. Various articles were brought to sell to me, and sometimes I had reason to rejoice at having stayed there. I was sure of a supper of milk and bread served in a wooden bowl, but whenever they supposed I should stay all night, they always killed a couple of fowls for me, which were baked in a small oven heated with pieces of mummy cases, and sometimes with the bones and rags of the mummies themselves. It is no uncommon thing to sit down near fragments of bones: hands, feet, or skulls, are often in the way, for these people are so accustomed to be among the mummies, that they think no more of sitting on them than on the skins of their dead calves. I also became indifferent about them at last and would have slept in a mummy pit as readily as out of it.

Here they appear to be contented. The laborer comes home in the evening, seats himself near his cave, smokes his pipe with his companions, and talks of the last inundation of the Nile, its products, and what the ensuing season is likely to be. His old wife brings him the usual bowl of lentils and bread moistened with water and salt, and (when she can add a little butter) it is a feast. Knowing nothing beyond this, he is happy. The young man's chief business is to accumulate the amazing sum of a hundred piastres (eleven dollars and ten cents) to buy himself a wife and to make a feast on the wedding-day.

If he has any children, they need no clothing: he leaves them to themselves till mother Nature pleases to teach them to work to gain money enough to buy a shirt or some other rag to cover themselves, for while they are children they are generally naked or covered with rags. The parents are roguishly cunning, and the children are schooled by their example, so that it becomes a matter of course to cheat strangers. Would anyone believe that, in such a state of life, luxury and ambition exist? If any woman be destitute of jewels, she is poor and looks with envy on one more fortunate than herself, who perhaps has the worth of half a crown round her neck. And she who has a few glass beads or some sort of coarse coral, a couple of silver brooches, or rings on her arms and legs, is considered as truly rich and great. Some of them are as complete coquettes, in their way, as any to be seen in the capitals of Europe.

When a young man wants to marry, he goes to the father of the intended bride and agrees with him what he is to pay for her. This being settled, so much money is to be spent on the wedding-day feast. To set up housekeeping, nothing is requisite but two or three earthen pots, a stone to grind meal, and a mat which is the bed. The spouse has a gown and jewels of her own, and if the bridegroom present her with a pair of bracelets of silver, ivory, or glass, she is happy and fortunate indeed.

The house is ready, without rent or taxes. No rain can pass through the roof, and there is no door, for there is no need of one, as there is nothing to lose. They make a kind of box of clay and straw, which, after two or three days' exposure to the sun, becomes quite hard. It is fixed on a stand, an aperture is left to put all their precious things into it, and a piece of mummy case forms the door. If the house does not please them, they walk out and enter another, as there are several hundreds at their command; I might say several thousands, but they are not all fit to receive inhabitants.

QUESTIONS — 1. Why did so few travelers succeed in reaching the bottom of the tombs? 2. What was Belzoni's purpose in exploring these tombs? 3. How did the people of Gournou, who lived in the tomb passageways, earn a livelihood? 4. What makes their homes somewhat eerie? 5. In that society with few possessions, had pride and jealousy been eradicated?

SPELL AND DEFINE — (1) separate, subterranean, inconven-

ience, sepulchers; (2) abyss, magnificent; (3) suffocating;
(4) commodious, converse, inured; (7) papyri, antiquities;
(8) horizontal, perpendicular; (10) appropriate, bandaged,
enamel; (13) companions, moisten, accumulate.

LESSON LXI (61)

Address to the Mummy
in Belzoni's Exhibition, London
NEW MONTHLY MAGAZINE

NOTE—In 1825, two years after Belzoni's death, his widow exhibited in Paris and London his drawings and models of the
royal tombs of Thebes. As Keats was inspired by a British
Museum exhibition of Greek classical sculpture to write "Ode
on a Grecian Urn," so the Belzoni Exhibition inspired an
unknown poet to pen the following poem.

And thou hast walk'd about (how strange a story!)
   In Thebes' streets three thousand years ago,
When the Memnonium was in all its glory,
   And time had not begun to overthrow
Those temples, palaces, and piles stupendous,
Of which the very ruins are tremendous.

Speak! for thou long enough has acted Dummy,
   Thou hast a tongue—come, let us hear its tune;
Thou'rt standing on thy legs, above ground, Mummy!
   Revisiting the glimpses of the moon,
Not like thin ghosts or disembodied creatures,
But with thy bones and flesh, and limbs and features.

Tell us—for doubtless thou canst recollect,
   To whom should we assign the sphinx's fame?
Was Cheops or Cephrenes architect

Of either pyramid that bears his name?
Is Pompey's pillar really a misnomer?
Had Thebes a hundred gates as sung by Homer?

Perhaps thou wert a Mason, and forbidden
  By oath to tell the mysteries of thy trade,
Then say what secret melody was hidden
  In Memnon's statue that at sunrise played?
Perhaps thou wert a Priest—if so, my struggles
Are vain;—Egyptian priests ne'er owned their juggles

Perchance that very hand, now pinioned flat,
  Has hobb-a-nobb'd with Pharoah glass to glass;
Or dropped a halfpenny in Homer's hat,
  Or doffed thine own to let Queen Dido pass,
Or held, by Solomon's own invitation,
A torch at the great Temple's dedication.

I need not ask thee if that hand, when armed,
  Has any Roman soldier mauled and knuckled,
For thou wert dead, and buried, and embalmed,
  Ere Romulus and Remus had been suckled:—
Antiquity appears to have begun
Long after thy primeval race was run.

Since first thy form was in this box extended,
  We have, above ground, seen some
        strange mutations;
The Roman empire has begun and ended;
  New worlds have risen—we have lost old nations,
And countless kings have into dust been humbled,
While not a fragment of thy flesh has crumbled.

Didst thou not hear the pother o'er thy head,
  When the great Persian conqueror, Cambyses,
March'd armies o'er thy tomb with thundering tread,
  O'erthrew Osiris, Orus, Apis, Isis,

And shook the pyramids with fear and wonder,
When the gigantic Memnon fell asunder?

If the tomb's secrets may not be confessed,
    The nature of thy private life unfold:—
A heart has throbb'd beneath that leathern breast,
    And tears adown that dusky cheek have rolled:—
Have children climb'd those knees,
        and kissed that face?
What was thy name and station, age and race?

Statue of flesh—immortal of the dead!
    Imperishable type of evanescence!
Posthumous man, who quitt'st thy narrow bed,
    And standest undecayed within our presence,
Thou wilt hear nothing till the Judgment morning
When the great trump shall thrill thee
        with its warning.

QUESTIONS — 1. In stanza one, what is credited with over-
throwing the ancient temples and palaces? 2. What do all of the
questions in stanza three have in common? 3. Identify the three
famous people from ancient times mentioned in stanza five:
Homer, Queen Dido, Solomon. 4. Throughout the poem, with
what does the poet contrast the comparatively unchanged form
of the mummy? 5. The poet realizes that all of his questions to
the mummy will go unanswered because it hears nothing. What
will be the first sound to penetrate the mummy's senses?

SPELL AND DEFINE — (1) stupendous; (2) glimpses; (3) pyramid, misnomer; (6) primeval; (7) mutations; (10) posthumous.

LESSON LXII (62)

The Fall of Babylon—BIBLE

NOTE—In the Bible, Babylon—both literal and symbolic—has long been identified as the traditional enemy of God's truth and people. In this selection from the Apocalypse (Revelation), the long awaited announcement is made: "Babylon is fallen." The translation and poetic arrangement used by McGuffey came from *Jebb's Sacred Literature.*

Revelation 18

And after these things, I saw another angel
    descending from heaven,
Having great power: and the earth was
    enlightened with his glory:
And he cried mightily with a loud voice: saying
She is fallen! she is fallen!
Babylon the great!
And is become the habitation of demons
And the hold of every impure spirit;
And the cage of every impure and hateful bird;
For in the wine of the wrath of her lewdness hath
    she pledged all nations;
And the kings of the earth have with her
    committed lewdness.
And the merchants of the earth, from the excess
    of her wanton luxury, have waxed rich;
And I heard another voice from heaven, saying:
Come out of her, my people;
That ye be not partakers of her sins,
And of her plagues that ye may not receive:
For her sins have reached up unto heaven,
And God hath remembered her iniquities:
Repay to her as she also hath repaid,

And double to her double, according to her works.
In the cup which she hath mingled,
    mingle to her double;
As much as she hath glorified herself and played
    the luxurious wanton,
So much give to her torment and sorrow:
For in her heart she saith,
"I sit a queen
And a widow am not I:
And sorrow I shall not see;"—
Therefore, in one day shall come her plagues;
Death, and mourning, and famine,
And with fire shall she be consumed;
For strong is the Lord God, who hath passed
    sentence upon her.
Then shall bewail her, and smite the breast for her,
The kings of the earth who have committed
Lewdness with her, and lived in wanton luxury,
When they shall see the smoke of her burning,
Standing afar off, because of the fear of her
    torment; saying,
"Woe! Woe! the great city, Babylon the strong city!
In one hour thy judgment is come!"
And the merchants of the earth shall weep and
    mourn over her,
For their merchandise no man buyeth any more:
Merchandise of gold and silver:
Of precious stones and pearls;
And of fine linen and of purple:
And of silk and scarlet;
And every odorous wood and every vessel of ivory;
And every vessel of most precious wood:
And of brass and iron and marble;
And cinnamon and amomum:
And perfumes, and myrrh, and incense;
And wine and oil;
And fine flour and wheat;

And cattle and sheep:
And horses and chariots and slaves;
And the souls of men:
And the autumnal fruits of thy soul's desire are
      gone from thee:
And all delicacies and splendors have vanished
      from thee,
And thou shalt never find them any more!
The merchants of these things, who were
      enriched by her,
Shall stand afar off because of the fear of her torment:
Weeping and mourning: saying,
"Woe! Woe! the great city!
She who was clothed in fine linen, and purple,
      and scarlet,
And was decked with gold, and precious stones,
      and pearls!
For in one hour is brought to desolation this so
      great wealth!"
And every ship-master, and every super-cargo,
And mariners, and all who labor on the sea,
Stood afar-off, and cried aloud,
When they saw the smoke of her burning; saying:
"What city, like the great city!"
And they cast dust upon their heads
And cried aloud, weeping and mourning; saying:
"Woe! Woe! the great city!
Wherein all who had ships upon the sea waxed rich
By her costliness;
For in one hour has she been made desolate!"
Rejoice over her thou heaven!
And ye saints! and ye apostles! and ye prophets!
For God hath for her crimes against you passed
      sentence upon her!
And a mighty angel took up a stone like a huge
      millstone, and cast it into the sea; saying:
"Thus with violence shall be thrown down

Babylon the great city, and shall be
 found no more;
And the voice of harpers, and musicians and flute
 players, and trumpeters shall be heard
 in thee no more
And any artificer of any ingenious art shall be
 found in thee no more:
And the sound of a millstone shall be heard in
 thee no more:
And the light of a lamp shall be seen in thee no more:
And the voice of the bridegroom, and of the bride,
 shall be heard in thee no more,
For thy merchants were the great ones of the earth;
For by thy sorceries were deceived all the nations,
And in her the blood of prophets and saints
 hath been found:
And of all those who were slain upon the earth."
And after these things I heard as it were the voice
 of a great multitude in heaven,
 saying, "Hallelujah!
Salvation, and glory, and honor
And power, be unto the Lord our God!
For true and righteous are his judgments;
For he hath judged the great harlot
Who corrupted the earth with her lewdness;
And he hath avenged the blood of her servants
 at her hand."
And, a second time they said, "Hallelujah!"
And her smoke ascendeth forever and ever!

QUESTIONS — 1. Who announces the downfall of Babylon?
2. What were Babylon's sins? 3. Who mourned over her downfall? Who rejoiced? 4. What tribute is given to God for His
righteous judgment against Babylon?

SPELL AND DEFINE—demons, hateful, merchants, iniquities, merchandise, cinnamon, perfumes, incense, desolation,
hallelujah.

LESSON LXIII (63)

On the Value of Studies—LORD BACON

NOTE—When Francis Bacon's famous collection of fifty-eight *Essays* was published in three installments (1597-1625), it met with immediate success. His was the first use of the essay as a literary form in England. Covering a wide variety of topics, the essays were written in a style that provided many "quotable quotes."

Studies serve for delight, for ornament, and for ability. Their chief use for delight, is in retired privacy; for ornament, in discourse; and for ability, in the arrangement and disposition of business: for expert men can execute, and, perhaps, judge of particulars, one by one; but general councils, and the plots and marshaling of affairs, come best from the learned. To spend too much time in studies, is sloth; to use them too much for ornament, is affectation; to form one's judgment wholly by their rules, is the humor of a scholar. They perfect nature, and are perfected by experience: for natural abilities are like natural plants, and need pruning by study; and studies themselves give forth directions too much at large, unless they are hedged in by experience.

Crafty men contemn studies; simple men admire, and wise men use them; for they teach not their own use, but that is a wisdom without them and above them, won by observation. Read not to contradict and confute; nor to believe or take for granted; nor to find matter merely for conversation; but to weigh and consider. Some books are to be tasted; others, to be swallowed; and some few, to be chewed and digested; that is, some books are to be only glanced at; others are to be read, but not critically; and some few are to be read wholly, and with diligence and attention. Some books, also, may be read by deputy, and extracts received from them which are made by others; but they should be only the meaner sort of books, and the less important arguments of those which are better: otherwise, distilled books are, like common, distilled waters, flashy things.

Reading makes a full man; conversation, a ready man; and writing, an exact man. Therefore, if a man write little, he needs a great memory; if he converse little, he wants a present wit; and, if he read little, he ought to have much cunning, that he may seem to know what he does not. History makes men wise; poetry makes them witty; mathematics, subtle; natural philosophy, deep; moral philosophy, grave; logic and rhetoric, able to contend: nay, there is no obstruction to the human faculties but what may be overcome by proper studies. Obstacles to learning, like the diseases of the body, are removed by appropriate exercises.

Thus, bowling is good for a weakness in the back; gunning, for the lungs and breast; walking, for the stomach; riding for the head, and the like; so, if one's thoughts are wandering, let him study mathematics; for, in demonstrating, if his attention be called away ever so little, he must begin again; if his faculties be not disciplined to distinguish and discriminate, let him study the schoolmen; for they are (*cymini sectores*) the cutters of cummin; if he is not accustomed to con over matters, and call up one fact with which to prove and illustrate another, let him study the lawyers' cases. Hence, every defect of the mind may have its special receipt.

There are three chief vanities in studies, by which learning has been most traduced; for we deem those things vain which are either false or frivolous— which have no truth, or are of no use; and those persons are considered vain, who are either credulous or curious. Judging, then, either from reason or experience, there prove to be three distempers of learning: the first is fantastical learning, the second, contentious learning, and the last, affected learning—vain imaginations, vain altercations, and vain affections.

QUESTIONS — 1. What, according to Bacon, are the chief uses of studies? 2. What does he consider their chief dangers? 3. Name several books that you feel should be (a) tasted (b) swallowed (c) digested. 4. What analogy does Bacon use to demonstrate that he thinks studies can correct problems with one's mental habits?

SPELL AND DEFINE — (1) ornament, ability, arrangement, councils, affection; (2) contemn, conversation; (4) mathematics, demonstrating; (5) frivolous, imaginations.

LESSON LXIV (64)

The Venomous Worm—JOHN RUSSELL

NOTE—To combat the serious social problems of drunkenness and alcoholism, an organized temperance movement developed in America in the early part of the 19th century. In 1826 the American Society for the Promotion of Temperance was founded in Boston; seven years later it had 6,000 local societies in several states with more than 1,000,000 members. This reform movement was heartily supported by the McGuffey READERS.

"——Outvenoms all the worms of Nile."

Who has not heard of the rattlesnake or copperhead? An unexpected sight of either of these reptiles will make even the lords of creation recoil, but there is a species of worm, found in various parts of this state, which conveys a poison of a nature so deadly, that, compared with it, even the venom of the rattlesnake is harmless. To guard our readers against this foe of human kind, is the object of this lesson.

This worm varies much in size. It is frequently an inch in diameter, but, as it is rarely seen, except when coiled, its length can hardly be conjectured. It is of a dull lead color and generally lives near a spring or small stream of water and bites the unfortunate people, who are in the *habit of going there to drink*. The brute creation it never molests. They avoid it with the same instinct that teaches the animals of Peru to shun the deadly coya.

Several of these reptiles have long infested our settlements, to the misery and destruction of many of our fellow citizens. I have, therefore, had frequent opportunities of being the melancholy spectator of the effects produced by the subtile poison which this worm infuses.

The symptoms of its *bite* are terrible. The eyes of the patient become red and fiery, his tongue swells to an immoderate size, and obstructs his utterance; and delirium of the most horrid character, quickly follows. Sometimes, in his madness, he attempts the destruction of his nearest friends.

If the sufferer has a family, his weeping wife and helpless infants are not unfrequently the objects of his frantic fury. In a word, he exhibits, to the life, all the detestable passions that rankle in the bosom of a savage; and, such is the *spell* in which his senses are locked, that, no sooner has the unhappy patient recovered from the paroxysm of insanity occasioned by the bite, than he seeks out the *destroyer*, for the sole purpose of being *bitten again*.

I have seen a good old father, his locks as white as snow, his step slow and trembling, beg in vain of

his only *son* to quit the lurking place of the worm.
My heart bled when he turned away; for I knew the
fond hope, that his son would be the "staff of his
declining years," had supported him through many
a sorrow.

Youths of America, would you know the name of
this reptile? It is called the *Worm of the Still.*

QUESTIONS — 1. What is the basic analogy made in this
lesson? 2. What group is never bothered by "the venomous
worm"? 3. Who, besides the victim, suffer from the bite of this
"worm"? 4. What part does the victim play in this tragedy?

SPELL AND DEFINE — (1) copperhead, venom; (2) conjecture, instinct; (3) infuses; (4) symptoms, utterance, delirium;
(5) exhibits, paroxysm; (6) lurking, declining.

LESSON LXV (65)

William Tell—KNOWLES

NOTE—William Tell was a legendary hero of Switzerland. His
story represents the spirit of the Swiss movement for independence from the Austrian Hapsburgs in the 1300's. According to
the *Encyclopaedia Britannica* (1968 ed., Vol. 21, p. 814), "there
is still no conclusive evidence for or against Tell's existence...."
A drama by Schiller and an opera by Rossini have given the
story worldwide renown.

Scene 1—*A mountain with mist. Gessler seen
descending with a hunting pole.*

Gessler. Alone—Alone! and every step the mist
Thickens around me! On these mountain tracks
To lose one's way, they say, is sometimes death!
What, ho! Holloa! No tongue replies to me!
What thunder hath the horror of this silence!

Cursed slaves, to let me wander from them!
　　Ho—Holloa!
My voice sounds weaker to mine ear; I've not
The strength to call I had; and through my limbs
Cold tremor runs—and sickening faintness seizes
On my heart. O, heaven, have mercy! Do not see
The color of the hands I lift to thee!
Look only on the strait wherein I stand,
And pity it! Let me not sink—Uphold!
Support me! Mercy! Mercy! *(He falls with faint-
ness. Albert enters, almost breathless with the
fury of the storm.)*

　　Albert.　I'll breathe upon this level, if the wind
Will let me. Ha! a rock to shelter me!
Thanks to it—a man! and fainting. Courage, friend!
Courage.—A stranger that has lost his way—
Take heart—take heart: you are safe.
　　　　How feel you now?

　　Ges.　Better.

　　Alb.　You have lost your way upon the hills?

　　Ges.　I have.

　　Alb.　And whither would you go?

　　Ges.　To Altorf.

　　Alb.　I'll guide you thither.

　　Ges.　You are a child.

　　Alb.　I know the way; the track I've come
Is harder far to find.

　　Ges.　The track you have come!
　　　—What mean you? Sure
You have not been still farther in the mountains?

　　Alb.　I have traveled from Mount Faigel.

　　Ges.　No one with thee?

　　Alb.　No one but Him.

　　Ges.　Do you not fear these storms?

　　Alb.　He's in the storm.

　　Ges.　And there are torrents, too,
That must be crossed?

Alb. He's by the torrent too.

Ges. You are but a child.

Alb. He will be with a child.

Ges. You are sure you know the way?

Alb. 'Tis but to keep the side of yonder stream.

Ges. But guide me safe, I'll give thee gold.

Alb. I'll guide thee safe without.

Ges. Here's earnest for thee.

Here—I'll double that,
Yea, treble it—but let me see the gate of Altorf.
Why do you refuse the gold? Take it.

Alb. No.

Ges. You shall.

Alb. I will not.

Ges. Why?

Alb. Because

I do not covet it;—and though I did,
It would be wrong to take it as the price
Of doing one a kindness.

Ges. Ha!—who taught thee that?

Alb. My father.

Ges. Does he live in Altorf?

Ges. No; in the mountains.

Ges. How—a mountaineer?

He should become a tenant of the city:
He would gain by it.

Alb. Not so much as he might lose by it.

Ges. What might he lose by it?

Alb. Liberty.

Ges. Indeed! He also taught thee that?

Alb. He did.

Ges. His name?

Alb. This is the way to Altorf, sir.

Ges. I would know thy father's name.

Alb. The day is wasting—we have far to go.

Ges. Thy father's name, I say?

Alb. I will not tell it thee.

Ges.   Not tell it me! Why?

Alb.   You may be an enemy of his.

Ges.   May be a friend.

Alb.   May be; but should you be
An enemy—although I would not tell you
My father's name—I would guide you safe to Altorf.
Will you follow me?

Ges.   Never mind thy father's name;
What would it profit me to know it? Thy hand;
We are not enemies.

Alb.   I never had an enemy.

Ges.   Lead on.

Alb.   Advance your staff
As you descend, and fix it well. Come on.

Ges.   What! must we take that steep?

Alb.   'Tis nothing! Come,
I'll go before. Never fear—come on! come on!
(Exeunt.)

Scene 2—The Gate of Altorf.
Enter Gessler and Albert.

Alb.   You are at the gate of Altorf.
     (Is returning.)

Ges.   Tarry, boy!

Alb.   I would be gone; I am waited for.

Ges.   Come back!
Who waits for thee? Come, tell me; I am rich
And powerful, and can reward.

Alb.   'Tis close
On evening; I have far to go; I'm late.

Ges.   Stay! I can punish, too.
Boy, do you know me?

Alb.   No.

Ges.   Why fear you, then,
To trust me with your father's name?—Speak.

Alb.   Why do you desire to know it?

Ges. You have served me,
And I would thank him, if I chanced to pass
His dwelling.

Alb. 'Twould not please him that a service
So trifling should be made so much of.

Ges. Trifling! You have saved my life.

Alb. Then do not question me,
But let me go.

Ges. When I have learned from thee
Thy father's name. What, ho! *(Knocks.)*

Sentinel. (Within.) Who's there?

Ges. Gessler. *(Soldiers enter.)*

Alb. Ha, Gessler!

Ges. (To the soldiers.)
Seize him. Wilt thou tell me
Thy father's name?

Alb. No.

Ges. I can bid them cast thee
Into a dungeon! Wilt thou tell it now?

Alb. No.

Ges. I can bid them strangle thee! Wilt tell it?

Alb. Never.

Ges. Away with him! Send Sarnem to me.
(Soldiers take Albert off.)

Behind that boy I see the shadow of
A hand must wear my fetters, or 'twill try
To strip me of my power. How I loathed the free
And fearless air with which he trod the hills!
I wished some way
To find the parent nest of this fine eaglet,
And harrow it! I'd like to clip the broad
And full grown wing that taught his tender pinion
So bold a flight. *(Enter Sarnem.)*
Ha, Sarnem! have the slaves
Attended me returned?

Sarnem. They have.

Ges.   You'll see
That every one of them be laid in fetters.
   Sar.   I will.
   Ges.   Did'st see that boy just now?
   Sar.   That passed me?
   Ges.   Yes.
   Sar.   A mountaineer.
   Ges.   You'd say so, saw you him
Upon the hills; he walks them like their lord!
I tell thee, Sarnem, looking on that boy,
I felt I was not master of those hills.
He has a father. Neither promises
Nor threats could draw from him his name—
         a father
Who talks to him of liberty. I fear that man.
   Sar.   He may be found.
   Ges.   He must—and soon
As found disposed of. I live
In danger till I find that man. Send parties
Into the mountains, to explore them far
And wide; and if they chance to light upon
A father, who expects his child, command them
To drag him straight before us.
         Sarnem, see it done.   *(Exeunt.)*

QUESTIONS — 1. Besides being an expression of kindness,
why was it wise of Albert to refuse payment for leading Gessler
to Altorf? 2. Why does Albert also refuse to reveal his father's
name? 3. What reason does Gessler give for wanting to know
Albert's father's name? 4. What is Gessler's real reason for
wanting to know the name of Albert's father?

SPELL AND DEFINE—tremor, breathe, mountaineer,
dungeon, eaglet, threats, straight.

LESSON LXVI (66)

William Tell—CONTINUED

Scene 3—*A chamber in the Castle.*
Enter Gessler, Officers, and Sarnem,
with Tell in chains and guarded.

Sar.   Down, slave! Behold the governor.
Down! down! and beg for mercy.
  Ges.   *(Seated.)*   Does he hear?
  Sar.   He does, but braves thy power.
  Officer.   Why don't you smite him for that look?
  Ges.   Can I believe
My eyes?—He smiles! Nay, grasps
His chains as he would make a weapon of them
To lay the smiter dead.   *(To Tell.)*
Why speakest thou not?
  Tell.   For wonder.
  Ges.   Wonder?
  Tell.   Yes, that thou should'st seem a man.
  Ges.   What should I seem?
  Tell.   A monster!
  Ges.   Ha! Beware—Think on thy chains.
  Tell.   Thought they were doubled, and did
        weigh me down
Prostrate to earth, methinks I could rise up—
Erect, with nothing but the honest pride
Of telling thee, usurper, to thy teeth,
Thou art a monster! Think upon my chains!
How came they on me?
  Ges.   Darest thou question me?
  Tell.   Darest thou not answer?
  Ges.   Do I hear?

Tell. Thou dost.

Ges. Beware my vengeance.

Tell. Can it more than kill?

Ges. Enough—it can do that.

Tell. No; not enough:
It cannot take away the grace of life—
Its comeliness of look that virtue gives—
Its port erect with consciousness of truth—
Its rich attire of honorable deeds—
Its fair report that's rife on good men's tongues:
It cannot lay its hands on these, no more
Than it can pluck the brightness from the sun,
Or with polluted finger tarnish it.

Ges. But it can make thee writhe.

Tell. It may.

Ges. And groan.

Tell. It may; and I may cry,
Go on, though it should make me groan again.

Ges. Whence comest thou?

Tell. From the mountains. Wouldst thou learn
What news from them?

Ges. Canst tell me any?

Tell. Ay; they watch no more the avalanche.

Ges. Why so?

Tell. Because they look for thee. The hurricane
Comes unawares upon them; from its bed,
The torrent breaks, and finds them in its track.

Ges. What do they then?

Tell. Thank heaven, it is not thou!
Thou hast perverted nature in them.
There's not a blessing heaven vouchsafes them, but
The thought of thee—doth wither to a curse.

Ges. That's right! I'd have them like their hills
That never smile, though wanton summer tempt
Them ever so much.

Tell. But they do sometimes smile.

Ges. Ay!—when is that?

Tell.   When they do talk of vengeance.

Ges.   Vengeance! Dare they talk of that?

Tell.   Ay, and expect it too.

Ges.   From whence?

Tell.   From heaven!

Ges.   From heaven?

Tell.   And their true hands
Are lifted up to it on every hill
For justice on thee.

Ges.   Where's thy abode?

Tell.   I told thee on the mountains.

Ges.   Art married?

Tell.   Yes.

Ges.   And hast a family?

Tell.   A son.

Ges.   A son! Sarnem!

Sar.   My lord, the boy. —*(Gessler signs to
Sarnem to keep silence, and, whispering, sends
him off.)*

Tell.   The boy!—what boy?
Is't mine?—and have they netted my young fledgling?
Now heaven support me, if they have! He'll own me,
And share his father's ruin! But a look
Would put him on his guard—yet how to give it!
Now, heart, thy nerve; forget thou art flesh, be rock.
They come—they come!
That step—that step—that little step, so light
Upon the ground, how heavy does it fall
Upon my heart! I feel my child! — *(Enter Sarnem
with Albert, whose eyes are riveted on Tell's bow,
which Sarnem carries.)*
'Tis he! —We can but perish.

Sar.   See!

Alb.   What?

Sar.   Look there!

Alb.   I do, what would you have me see?

Sar.   Thy father.

Alb. Who? That—that my father!

Tell. My boy—my boy! —my own brave boy!
He's safe! *(Aside.)*

Sar. (Aside to Gessler.)
They're like each other.

Ges. Yet I see no sign
Or recognition to betray the link
Unites a father and his child.

Sar. My lord.
I am sure it is his father. Look at them.
It may be
A preconcerted thing 'gainst such a chance,
That they survey each other coldly thus.

Ges. We shall try. Lead forth the caitiff.

Sar. To a dungeon?

Ges. No; into the court.

Sar. The court, my lord?

Ges. And send
To tell the headsman to make ready. Quick!
The slave shall die! —You marked the boy?

Sar. I did. He started—'tis his father.

Ges. We shall see. Away with him!

Tell. Stop! —Stop!

Ges. What would you?

Tell. Time! A little time to call my
thoughts together.

Ges. Thou shalt not have a minute.

Tell. Someone, then, to speak with.

Ges. Hence with him!

Tell. A moment! —Stop!
Let me speak to the boy.

Ges. Is he thy son?

Tell. And if
He were, art thou so lost to nature, as
To send me forth to die before his face?

Ges. Well! speak with him.
Now, Sarnem, mark them well.

Tell. Thou dost not know me, boy—
    and well for thee
Thou dost not. I'm the father of a son
About thy age. Thou,
I see, wast born like him upon the hills;
If thou should'st 'scape thy present thraldom, he
May chance to cross thee; if he should, I pray thee
Relate to him what has been passing here,
And say I laid my hand upon thy head,
And said to thee—if he were here, as thou art,
Thus would I bless him. Mayest thou live, my boy!
To see thy country free, or die for her,
As I do! *(Albert weeps.)*
  Sar. Mark! he weeps.
  Tell. Were he my son,
He would not shed a tear! He would remember
The cliff where he was bred, and learned to scan
A thousand fathoms' depth of nether air;
Where he was trained to hear the thunder talk,
And meet the lightning eye to eye—where last
We spoke together—when I told him death
Bestowed the brightest gem that graces life—
Embraced for virtue's sake—He shed a tear!
Now were he by I'd talk to him, and his cheek
Should never blanch, nor moisture dim his eye—
I'd talk to him—
  Sar. He falters!
  Tell. 'Tis too much!
And yet it must be done! I'd talk to him—
  Ges. Of what?
  Tell. The mother, tyrant, thou dost make
A widow of! —I'd talk to him of her.
I'd bid him tell her, next to liberty,
Her name was the last word my lips pronounced.
And I would charge him never to forget
To love and cherish her, as he would have
His father's dying blessing rest upon him!

Sar. You see, as he doth prompt the other acts.

Tell. So well he bears it, he doth vanquish me.
My boy—my boy! —O for the hills, the hills,
To see him bound along their tops again,
With liberty.

Sar. Was there not all the father in that look?

Tell. Yet 'tis 'gainst nature.

Sar. Not if he believes
To own the son would be to make him share
The father's death.

Ges. I did not think of that! —'Tis well
The boy is not thy son—I've destined him
To die along with thee.

Tell. To die? —For what?

Ges. For having braved my power,
  as thou hast. Lead
Them forth.

Tell. He's but a child.

Ges. Away with them!

Tell. Perhaps an only child.

Ges. No matter.

Tell. He may have a mother.

Ges. So the viper hath;
And yet, who spares it for the mother's sake?

Tell. I talk to stone! I talk to it as though
'Twere flesh; and know 'tis none. I'll talk to it
No more. Come, my boy—
I taught thee how to live—I'll show thee
  how to die.

Ges. He is thy child?

Tell. He is my child.

Ges. I've wrung a tear from him! Thy name!

Tell. My name?
It matters not to keep if from thee now;
My name is Tell.

Ges. Tell! —William Tell?

Tell. The same.

Ges. What! he, so famed 'bove all his countrymen
For guiding o'er the stormy lake the boat?
And such a master of his bow, 'tis said
His arrows never miss! —Indeed—I'll take
Exquisite vengeance! —Mark! I'll spare thy life—
Thy boy's too—both of you are free—on one
Condition.

Tell. Name it.

Ges. I would see you make
A trial of your skill with that same bow
You shoot so well with.

Tell. Name the trial you
Would have me make.

Ges. You look upon your boy
As though instinctively you guessed it.

Tell. Look upon my boy!
    —What mean you? Look upon
My boy as though I guessed it?
    —Guessed the trial
You'd have to make! —Guessed it
Instinctively! You do not mean—No—no—
You would not have me make a trial of
My skill upon my child! —Impossible!
I do not guess your meaning.

Ges. I would see
Thee hit an apple at the distance of
A hundred paces.

Tell. Is my boy to hold it?

Ges. No.

Tell. No! —I'll send the arrow through the core!

Ges. It is to rest upon his head.

Tell. Great heaven, you hear him!

Ges. Thou dost hear the choice I give—
Such trial of the skill thou art master of,
Or death to both of you; not otherwise
To be escaped.

Tell. O, monster!

Ges.   Wilt thou do it?

Alb.   He will! he will!

Tell.   Ferocious monster! —Make
A father murder his own child.

Ges.   Take off
His chains if he consent.

Tell.   With his own hand!

Ges.   Does he consent?

Alb.   He does.   *(Gessler signs to his officers,
who proceed to take off Tell's chains; Tell all the
time unconscious what they do.)*

Tell.   With his own hand!
Murder his child with his own hand—This hand!
The hand I've led him, when an infant, by!—
'Tis beyond horror— 'tis most horrible.
Amazement!   *(His chains fall off.)*
What's that you've done to me?
Villains! put on my chains again. My hands
Are free from blood, and have no gust for it,
That they should drink my child's! Here! here! I'll not
Murder my boy for Gessler.

Alb.   Father—Father!—
You will not hit me, father!—

Tell.   Hit thee! Send
The arrow through thy brain—or, missing that,
Shoot out an eye—or, if thine eye escape,
Mangle the cheek I've seen thy mother's lips
Cover with kisses!—Hit thee—hit a hair
Of thee, and cleave thy mother's heart—

Ges.   Dost thou consent?

Tell.   Give me my bow and quiver.

Ges.   For what?

Tell.   —To shoot my boy!

Alb.   No—father—no!
To save me! —you'll be sure to hit the apple—
Will you not save me, father?

Tell. Lead me forth—
I'll make the trial!
   Alb. Thank you!
   Tell. Thank me? Do
You know for what? —I will not make the trial,
To take him to his mother in my arms,
And lay him down a corpse before her!
   Ges. Then he dies this moment—and you certainly
Do murder him whose life you have a chance
To save, and will not use it.
   Tell. Well—I'll do it: I'll make the trial.
   Alb. Father—
   Tell. Speak not to me:
Let me not hear thy voice—Thou must be dumb;
And so should all things be—Earth should be dumb;
And heaven—unless its thunders muttered at
The deed, and sent a bolt to stop it! —Give me
My bow and quiver!
   Ges. When all's ready.
   Tell. Well—Lead on!

QUESTIONS — 1. Gessler, as the Austrian Governor, represented the domination of Austria over Switzerland. What personal characteristics protrayed by the writer help to make Gessler the villain? 2. What personal characteristics help to make Tell the hero? 3. Why is there discontent among the people in the mountains? 4. What ruse did William Tell use to get a message to his son? 5. Why did Tell finally confess that Albert was his son? 6. On what condition did Gessler offer to spare the lives of William and Albert?

SPELL AND DEFINE — avalanche, hurricane, vouchsafe, wanton, vengeance, fledgling, perish, thraldom, liberty, exquisite, instinctively.

LESSON LXVII (67)

William Tell—CONCLUDED

Scene 4—*Enter slowly, people in evident distress—
Officers, Sarnem, Gessler, Tell, Albert, and
soldiers—one bearing Tell's bow and
quiver—another with a basket of apples.*

    Ges.   That is your ground. Now shall they
measure thence
A hundred paces. Take the distance.
    Tell. Is the line a true one?
    Ges.   True or not, what is't to thee?
    Tell. What is't to me? —A little thing,
A very little thing—a yard to two
Is nothing here or there—were it a wolf
I shot at! —Never mind.
    Ges.   Be thankful, slave.
Our grace accords thee life on any terms.
    Tell. I will be thankful, Gessler! —Villain, stop!
You measure to the sun.
    Ges.   And what of that?
What matter whether to or from the sun?
    Tell.   I'd have it at my back—The sun should shine
Upon the mark, and not on him that shoots.
I cannot see to shoot against the sun—
I will not shoot against the sun!
    Ges.   Give him his way! Thou hast cause to
       bless my mercy.
    Tell.   I shall remember it. I'd like to see
The apple I'm to shoot at.
    Ges.   Stay! show me the basket! —there—
    Tell.   You've picked the smallest one.
    Ges.   I know I have.

Tell. O! do you? —But you see
The color on't is dark—I'd have it light,
To see it better.

Ges. Take it as it is:
Thy skill will be the greater if thou hitt'st it.

Tell. True—true! —I did not think of that—
    I wonder
I did not think of that—Give me some chance
To save my boy!

        (Throws away the apple with all his force.)
        I will not murder him,
If I can help it—for the honor of
The form thou wearest, if all the heart is gone.

Ges. Well: choose thyself.

Tell. Have I a friend among the lookers on?

Verner. *(Rushing forward.)* Here, Tell!

Tell. I thank thee, Verner!
He is a friend runs out into a storm
To shake a hand with us. I must be brief.
When once the bow is bent, we cannot take
The shot too soon. Verner, whatever be
The issue of this hour, the common cause
Must not stand still. Let not tomorrow's sun
Set on the tyrant's banner! Verner! Verner!
The boy! —the boy! —Thinkest thou
        he hath the courage
To stand it?

Ver. Yes.

Tell. Does he tremble?

Ver. No.

Tell. Art sure?

Ver. I am.

Tell. How looks he?

Ver. Clear and smilingly.
If you doubt it—look yourself.

Tell. No—no—my friend;
To hear it is enough.

Ver. He bears himself so much above his years—

Tell. I know! —I know.

Ver. With constancy so modest—

Tell. I was sure he would—

Ver. And looks with such relying love
And reverence upon you—

Tell. Man! —Man! —Man!
No more! Already I'm too much the father
To act the man! —Verner, no more, my friend!
I would be flint—flint—flint. Don't make me feel
I'm not—do not mind me! Take the boy
And set him, Verner, with his back to me.
Set him upon his knees—and place this apple
Upon his head, so that the stem may front me,
Thus, Verner; charge him to keep steady—tell him
I'll hit the apple! —Verner, do all this
More briefly than I tell it thee.

Ver. Come, Albert! *(Leading him out.)*

Alb. May I not speak with him before I go?

Ver. No.

Alb. I would only kiss his hand.

Ver. You must not.

Alb. I must! —I cannot go from him without.

Ver. It is his will you should.

Alb. His will is it?
I am content then—come.

Tell. My boy! *(Holding out his arms to him.)*

Alb. My father! *(Rushing into Tell's arms.)*

Tell. If thou canst bear it, should not I? —Go now,
My son—and keep in mind that I can shoot—
Go boy—Be thou but steady, I will hit
The apple—Go!—God bless thee—go. —My bow!
        (The bow is handed to him.)
Thou wilt not fail thy master, wilt thou? —thou
Hast never failed him yet, old servant—No,
I'm sure of thee—I know thy honesty,
Thou art staunch—staunch. —Let me see my quiver.

Ges. Give him a single arrow.

Tell. Do you shoot?

Soldier. I do.

Tell. Is it so you pick an arrow, friend?
The point you see is bent; the feather jagged—
    (Breaks it.)
That's all the use 'tis fit for.

Ges. Let him have another.

Tell. Why 'tis better than the first,
But yet not good enough for such an aim
As I'm to take—'Tis heavy in the shaft;
I'll not shoot with it! *(Throws it away.)*
Let me see my quiver.
Bring it!—'Tis not one arrow in a dozen
I'd take to shoot with at a dove, much less
A dove like that.—

Ges. It matter not.
Show him the quiver.

Tell. See if the boy is ready.
    (Tell here hides an arrow under his vest.)

Ver. He is.

Tell. I'm ready too! Keep silent for
Heav'n's sake, and do not stir—and let me have
Your prayers—your prayers—and be my witnesses
That if his life's in peril from my hand,
'Tis only for the chance of saving it.
    (To the people.)

Ges. Go on.

Tell. I will.
O friends, for mercy's sake, keep motionless
And silent. *(Tell shoots—a shout of exultation
bursts from the crowd. Tell's head drops on his
bosom; he with difficulty supports himself upon
his bow.)*

Ver. (Rushing in with Albert.) Thy boy is
    safe, no hair of him is touched.

Alb.   Father, I'm safe—Your Albert's safe,
     dear father,—
Speak to me! Speak to me!
  Ver.   He cannot, boy!
  Alb.   You grant him life?
  Ges.   I do.
  Alb.   And we are free?
  Ges.   You are.   *(Crossing angrily behind.)*
  Alb.   Thank heaven! —thank heaven!
  Ver.   Open his vest,
And give him air.   *(Albert opens his father's vest,
and the arrow drops. Tell starts—fixes his eye on
Albert, and clasps him to his breast.)*
  Tell.   My boy! —My boy!
  Ges.   For what
Hid you that arrow in your breast? —Speak, slave!
  Tell.   To kill thee, tyrant, had I slain my boy!

QUESTIONS — 1. What request by Tell concerning the trial
arrangement does Gessler grant? 2. What message does Tell
give to his friend Verner? 3. Why is Albert able to remain calm
and stoic? 4. How does Tell manage to have his quiver brought
to him? Why? 5. What was the purpose of the hidden arrow?

SPELL AND DEFINE—tyrant, villain, servant, quiver,
prayer, witnesses.

LESSON LXVIII (68)

The Proverbs of Solomon—BIBLE

NOTE—King Solomon, the son of David, wrote the Proverbs early in his reign while he still followed the way of the Lord. The Proverbs exalt wisdom, which is defined as "the fear of the Lord." Much of the instruction is ethical and moral rather than spiritual.

A wise son maketh a glad father:
But a foolish son is the heaviness of his mother.
Treasures of wickedness profit nothing:
But righteousness delivereth from death.
The Lord will not suffer the soul of the
righteous to famish:
But he casteth away the substance of the wicked.
He becometh poor that dealeth with a slack hand:
But the hand of the diligent maketh rich.
He that gathereth in summer is a wise son:
But he that sleepeth in harvest
is a son that causeth shame.
Blessings are upon the head of the just:
But violence covereth the mouth of the wicked.
The memory of the just is blessed:
But the name of the wicked shall rot.
The wise in heart will receive commandments:
But a prating fool shall fall.
He that walketh uprightly walketh surely:
But he that perverteth his ways shall be known.
He that winketh with the eye causeth sorrow:
But a prating fool shall fall.
The mouth of a righteous man is a well of life:
But violence covereth the mouth of the wicked.
Hatred stirreth up strifes:
But love covereth all sins.

In the lips of him that hath understanding
    wisdom is found:
But a rod is for the back of him that is
    void of understanding.
  Wise men lay up knowledge:
But the mouth of the foolish is near destruction.
  The rich man's wealth is his strong city:
The destruction of the poor is their poverty.
  The labor of the righteous tendeth to life:
The fruit of the wicked to sin.
  He is in the way of life that keepeth instruction:
But he that refuseth reproof erreth.
  He that hideth hatred with lying lips,
And he that uttereth a slander, is a fool.
  In the multitude of words there wanteth not sin:
But he that refraineth his lips is wise.
  The tongue of the just is as choice silver:
The heart of the wicked is little worth.
  The lips of the righteous feed many:
But fools die for want of wisdom.
  The blessing of the Lord, it maketh rich,
And he addeth no sorrow with it.
  It is as sport to a fool to do mischief:
But a man of understanding hath wisdom.
  The fear of the wicked, it shall come upon him:
But the desire of the righteous shall be granted.
  As the whirlwind passeth, so is the wicked no more:
But the righteous is an everlasting foundation.
  As vinegar to the teeth, and as smoke to the eyes,
So is the sluggard to them that send him.
  The fear of the Lord prolongeth days:
But the years of the wicked shall be shortened.
  The hope of the righteous shall be gladness:
But the expectation of the wicked shall perish.
  The way of the Lord is strength to the upright:
But destruction shall be to the workers of iniquity.
  The righteous shall never be removed:

But the wicked shall not inhabit the earth.

The mouth of the just bringeth forth wisdom:
But the froward tongue shall be cut out.

The lips of the righteous know what is acceptable:
But the mouth of the wicked speaketh frowardness.

QUESTIONS — 1. In this selection how many lines constitute a single proverb? 2. How do these proverbs teach by *contrast?* 3. Select a proverb and write an essay developing its theme.

SPELL AND DEFINE — wickedness, heaviness, memory, receive, reproof, slander, tongue, whirlwind, inhabit.

LESSON LXIX (69)

Ladies' Head Dresses—SPECTATOR

NOTE—In the 1700s women's hairstyles were extremely high (many measuring more than two feet) and had to be held up with wire frames. They were decorated with feathers, ribbons, jewels and other ornaments. So complicated were these hairstyles, that women sometimes did not wash or comb their hair for weeks. In a literary style that was popularized by the SPECTATOR, the writer of this selection makes witty and satirical comments about the changing hair fashions.

There is not so variable a thing in nature as a lady's headdress: within my own memory, I have known it to rise and fall above thirty degrees. About ten years ago, it shot up to a very great height, insomuch that the female part of our species were much taller than the men. The women were of such an enormous stature, that we appeared as grasshoppers before them. At present the whole sex is in a manner dwarfed and shrunk into a race of beauties that seem almost another species.

I remember several ladies who were once very near seven feet high, that at present lack some inches of five. How they came to be thus curtailed, I cannot learn. Whether the whole sex be at present under any penance, which we know nothing of; or whether they have cast their headdresses in order to surprise us with something of that kind which shall be entirely new; or whether some of the tallest of the sex, being too cunning for the rest, have contrived this method to make themselves appear sizeable, is still a secret. Though I find some are of opinion, they are at present like trees new lopped and pruned, that will certainly sprout up and flourish with greater heads than before.

For my own part, as I do not love to be insulted by women who are taller than myself, I admire the sex much more in their present humiliation, which has reduced them to their natural dimensions, than when they had extended their persons, and lengthened themselves out into formidable and gigantic figures. I am not for adding to the beautiful edifices of nature, not for raising any whimsical superstructure upon her plans: I must therefore repeat it, that I am highly pleased with the coiffure now in fashion, and think it shows the good sense which at present very much reigns among the valuable part of the sex. One may observe that women in all ages have taken more pains than men to adorn the outside of their heads, and indeed I very much admire, that those architects, who raise such wonderful structures out of ribbons, lace, and wire have not been recorded for their respective inventions. It is certain that there have been as many orders in these kinds of buildings, as in those which have been made of marble. Sometimes they rise in the shape of a pyramid, sometimes like a tower, and sometimes like a steeple.

In Juvenal's time, the building grew by several orders and stories, as he has very humorously described it.

With curls on curls they build her head before,
And mount it with a formidable tower.

But I do not remember, in any part of my reading, that the headdress aspired to such an extravagance as in the fourteenth century, when it was built up in a couple of cones or spires which stood so excessively high on each side of the head, that a woman who was but a pigmy without her headdress appeared like a colossus upon putting it on. Monsieur Paradin says, "That these old-fashioned fontages rose one ell* above the head; that they were pointed like steeples, and had long loose pieces of crepe fastened to the tops of them, which were curiously fringed, and hung down their backs like streamers."

The women might possibly have carried this Gothic building much higher, had not a famous monk, Thomas Connecte by name, attacked it with great zeal and resolution. This holy man traveled from place to place to preach down this monstrous commode; and succeeded so well in it, that, as the magicians sacrificed their books to the flames upon the preaching of an apostle, many of the women threw down their headdresses in the middle of his sermon, and made a bonfire of them within sight of the pulpit. He was so renowned, as well for sanctity of his life, as his manner of preaching, that he had often a congregation of twenty thousand people; the men placing themselves on the one side of the pulpit, and the women on the other, they appeared, to use the similitude of an ingenious writer, like a forest of cedars with their heads reaching to the clouds.

He so warmed and animated the people against

this monstrous ornament, that it lay under a kind of persecution; and whenever it appeared in public, was pelted down by the rabble, who flung stones at the persons that wore it. But notwithstanding this prodigy vanished while the preacher was among them, it began to appear again some months after his departure, or, to tell it in Monsieur Paradin's own words, "The women, that, like snails in a fright, had drawn in their horns, shot them out again as soon as the danger was over."

It is usually observed, that a good reign is the only proper time for the making of laws against the exorbitance of power. In the same manner an excessive headdress may be attacked the most effectually when the fashion is against it. I do therefore recommend this paper to my female readers by way of prevention.

I would desire the fair sex to consider how impossible it is for them to add anything that can be ornamental to what is already the masterpiece of nature. The head has the most beautiful appearance, as well as the highest station, in the human figure. Nature has laid out all her art in beautifying the face. She has touched it with vermillion, planted in it a double row of ivory, made it the seat of smiles and blushes, lighted it up and enlivened it with the brightness of the eyes, hung it on each side with curious organs of sense, given it airs and graces that cannot be described, and surrounded it with such a flowing shade of hair, as sets all its beauties in the most agreeable light: in short, she seems to have designed the head as the cupola to the most glorious of her works, and when we load it with such a pile of supernumerary ornaments, we destroy the symmetry of the human figure and foolishly contrive to call off the eye from great and real beauties, to childish gewgaws, ribbons and bone-lace.

*A former English unit of length equal to 45 inches.

QUESTIONS — 1. When the women wore the extremely high hairstyles, how did the men appear next to them? 2. Why does the writer prefer hairstyles of "natural dimensions"? 3. How did the preaching of the monk Thomas Connecte influence the women? 4. At the time this essay was written, the high coiffure had just recently gone out of vogue. Why did the writer then bother to criticize the high styles?

SPELL AND DEFINE — (1) degrees, enormous; (2) curtailed; (3) humiliation, edifices, gigantic, coiffure; (4) humorously, colossus, extravagance; (5) commode, sanctity, similitude; (8) masterpiece.

LESSON LXX (70)

Ginevra—ROGERS

NOTE—"Ginevra" is part of a long poem entitled *Italy*, one of the most popular poems during the early 1800s. The poet Samuel Rogers wrote regarding the plot, "This story is, I believe, founded on fact; though time and place are uncertain. Many of the houses in England lay claim to it." (Lindberg, pp. 136, 138.)

If ever you should come to Modena,
Stop at a palace near the Reggio gate,
Dwelt in of old by one of the Donati.
Its noble gardens, terrace above terrace,
And rich in fountains, statues, cypresses,
Will long detain you; but, before you go,
Enter the house—forget it not, I pray you—
And look awhile upon a picture there.

'Tis of a lady in her earliest youth,
The last of that illustrious family;
Done by Zampieri; but by whom I care not.

He, who observes it, ere he passes on,
Gazes his fill, and comes and comes again.
That he may call it up when far away.

She sits, inclining forward as to speak,
Her lips half open, and her finger up,
As though she said, "Beware!" her vest of gold
Broidered with flowers, and clasped from head to foot,
An emerald stone in every golden clasp;
And on her brow, fairer than alabaster,
A coronet of pearls.

But then her face,
So lovely, yet so arch, so full of mirth,
The overflowings of an innocent heart;
It haunts me still, though many a year has fled,
Like some wild melody!

Alone it hangs
Over a moldering heirloom; its companion,
An oaken chest, half eaten by the worm,
But richly carved by Antony of Trent,
With scripture stories from the life of Christ;
A chest that came from Venice, and had held
The ducal robes of some old ancestors—
That by the way, it may be true or false—
But don't forget the picture; and you will not,
When you have heard the tale they told me there.

She was an only child, her name Ginevra,
The joy, the pride of an indulgent father;
And in her fifteenth year became a bride,
Marrying an only son, Francesco Doria,
Her playmate from her birth, and her first love.

Just as she looks there, in her bridal dress,
She was all gentleness, all gayety,

Her pranks the favorite theme of every tongue.
But now the day was come, the day, the hour;
Now, frowning, smiling for the hundredth time,
The nurse, that ancient lady, preached decorum;
And, in the luster of her youth, she gave
Her hand, with her heart in it, to Francesco.

Great was the joy; but at the nuptial feast,
When all sat down, the bride herself was wanting;
Nor was she to be found! Her father cried,
" 'Tis but to make a trial of our love!"
And filled his glass to all; but his hand shook,
And soon from guest to guest the panic spread.

'Twas but that instant she had left Francesco,
Laughing and looking back and flying still,
Her ivory tooth imprinted on his finger.
But now, alas! she was not to be found;
Nor from that hour could anything be guessed,
But that she was not!

      Weary of his life,
Francesco flew to Venice, and embarking,
Flung it away in battle with the Turk.
Donati lived; and long might you have seen
An old man wandering as in quest of something,
Something he could not find, he knew not what.
When he was gone, the house remained awhile
Silent and tenantless; then went to strangers.

Full fifty years were past, and all forgotten,
When on an idle day, a day of search
'Mid the old lumber in the gallery,
That moldering chest was noticed; and 'twas said
By one as young, as thoughtless as Ginevra,
"Why not remove it from its lurking place?"
'Twas done as soon as said; but on the way

It burst, it fell; and lo! a *skeleton*,
With here and there a pearl, an emerald stone,
A golden clasp, clasping a shred of gold.
All else has perished, save a wedding ring,
And a small seal, her mother's legacy,
Engraven with a name, the name of both;
"Ginevra."

—There then had she found a grave:
Within that chest had she concealed herself,
Fluttering with joy, the happiest of the happy;
When a springlock, that lay in ambush there,
Fastened her down forever!

QUESTIONS — 1. The poet says that several "houses in England lay claim" to the story. In his poem, however, he moved the setting to what country? 2. What treasure in the palace at Modena attracts the attention of all visitors? 3. What tragedy happened to Ginevra on her wedding day? 4. How long was it before the mystery was solved?

SPELL AND DEFINE — (1) fountains, statues; (2) illustrious; (4) haunts, melody; (5) moldering, ancestors; (7) bridal; (8) nuptial, panic; (9) imprint; (10) embarking; (11) lumber, skeleton; (12) concealed, springlock.

LESSON LXXI (71)

Reflections in Westminster Abbey
ADDISON

NOTE—Westminster Abbey in London is a great national shrine and the burial place of Britain's honored dead. All, except two, of the English rulers from William the Conqueror to Elizabeth II have been crowned there. Kings and queens, political leaders, poets, and other important people are buried in various parts of the Abbey.

When I am in a serious humor, I very often walk by myself in Westminster Abbey, where the gloominess of the place and the use to which it is applied, with the solemnity of the building and the condition of the people who lie in it, are apt to fill the mind with a kind of melancholy, or rather thoughtfulness, that is not disagreeable. I yesterday passed a whole afternoon in the churchyard, the cloisters, and the church amusing myself with the tombstones and inscriptions which I met with in those several regions of the dead.

Most of them recorded nothing else of the buried person, but that he was born upon one day and died upon another. The whole history of his life being comprehended in these two circumstances that are common to all mankind. I could not but look upon those registers of existence, whether of brass or marble, as a kind of satire upon the departed persons, who had left no other memorial of themselves, but that they were born, and that they died.

Upon my going into the church, I entertained myself with the digging of a grave and saw, in every shovelfull of it that was thrown up, the fragment of a bone or skull, intermixed with a kind of fresh mouldering earth that, some time or other, had a place in the composition of a human body. Upon this, I began to consider with myself, what innumerable multitudes of people lay confused together under the pavements of that ancient cathedral; how men and women, friends and enemies, priests and soldiers, monks and prebendaries were crumbled amongst one another and blended together in the same common mass; how beauty, strength, and youth with old age, weakness, and deformity lay undistinguished in the same promiscuous heap of matter.

After having thus surveyed this great magazine of mortality as it were in the lump, I examined it more particularly by the accounts which I found on several of the monuments which are raised in every quarter of that ancient fabric. Some of them were covered with such extravagant epitaphs that, if it were possible for the dead person to be acquainted with them, he would blush at the praises which his friends have bestowed upon him. There are others so excessively modest, that they deliver the character of the person departed in Greek or Hebrew, and by that means are not understood once in a twelvemonth. In the poetical quarter, I found that there were poets who had no monuments, and monuments which had no poets. I observed, indeed, that the present war had filled the church with many of those uninhabited monuments, which had been erected to the memory of persons whose bodies were perhaps buried in the plains of Blenheim or in the bosom of the ocean.

I could not but be very much delighted with several modern epitaphs, which are written with great elegance of expression and justness of thought and which therefore do honor to the living as well as the dead. As a foreigner is very apt to conceive an idea of the ignorance of politeness of a nation from the turn of their public monuments and inscriptions, they should be submitted to the perusal of men of learning and genius, before they are put into execution. Sir Cloudesley Shovel's monument has very often given me great offence. Instead of the brave rough English admiral which was the distinguishing character of that plain gallant man, he is represented on his tomb by the figure of a beau, dressed in a long periwig, and reposing himself upon velvet cushions under a canopy of state.

The inscription is answerable to the monument, for, instead of celebrating the many remarkable actions he had performed in the service of his country, it acquaints us only with the manner of his death, in which it was impossible for him to reap any honor. The Dutch, whom we are apt to despise for want of genius, show an infinitely greater taste in their buildings and works of this nature, than we meet with in those of our own country. The monuments of their admirals, which have been erected at the public expense, represent them like themselves, and are adorned with rostral crowns and naval ornaments, with beautiful festoons of sea-weed, shells, and coral.

I know that entertainments of this nature are apt to raise dark and dismal thoughts in timorous minds and gloomy imaginations, but for my own part, though I am always serious, I do not know what it is to be melancholy and can therefore take a view of nature in her deep and solemn scenes with the same pleasure as in her most gay and delightful ones. By these means I can improve myself with objects which others consider with terror.

When I look upon the tombs of the great, every emotion of envy dies in me; when I read the epitaphs of the beautiful, every inordinate desire goes out; when I meet with the grief of parents upon a tombstone, my heart melts with compassion; when I see the tomb of parents themselves, I consider the vanity of grieving for those whom we must quickly follow. When I see kings lying by those who deposed them; when I consider rival wits placed side by side, or the holy men that divided the world with their contests and disputes; I reflect with sorrow and astonishment on the little competitions, factions, and debates of mankind. When I read the several dates of the tombs, of some that died yesterday, and some six hundred years ago, I consider that great day when we shall all of us be contemporaries and make our appearance together.

QUESTIONS — 1. What did Addison learn from watching the grave diggers? 2. Why does an inscription in Greek or Hebrew make an unsatisfactory epitaph? 3. In the final paragraph Addison relates his thoughts and feelings as he looks upon the tombs of various kinds of people. What does he think of when he sees the tombs of those who died yesterday and the tombs of those who died 600 years ago?

SPELL AND DEFINE — (1) cloister, inscriptions; (4) epitaph, blush, monument; (6) genius, rostral, festoons; (8) contemporaries.

LESSON LXXII (72)

America's Contributions to Europe
WEBSTER

NOTE—This lesson is an extract from an address delivered
June 17, 1843, by Daniel Webster at the celebration of the com-
pletion of the Bunker Hill Monument. Built on Breed's Hill in
the Charlestown section of Boston, the monument honors one of
the early battles of the Revolutionary War.

Few topics are more inviting or more fit for philosophical discussion, than the action and influence of
the New World upon the Old, or the contributions of
America to Europe.

Her obligations to Europe for science and art,
laws, literature, and manners America acknowl-
edges as she ought, with respect and gratitude. And
the people of the United States, descendants of the
English stock, grateful for the treasures of knowledge derived from their English ancestors, acknowledge, also, with thanks and filial regard, that among
those ancestors, under the culture of Hampden and
Sidney and other assiduous friends, that seed of
popular liberty first germinated, which on our soil
has shot up to its full height until its branches over-
shadow all the land.

But America has not failed to make returns. If
she has not canceled the obligation or equaled it by
others of like weight, she has, at least, made respectable advances, and some approaches toward
equality. And she admits that standing in the midst
of civilized nations and in a civilized age, a nation
among nations, there is a high part which she is ex-

pected to act, for the general advance of human interests and human welfare.

American mines have filled the mints of Europe with the precious metals. The productions of the American soil and climate have poured out their abundance of luxuries for the tables of the rich and of necessaries for the sustenance of the poor. Birds and animals of beauty and value have been added to the European stocks, and transplantations from the transcendent and unequaled riches of our forests have mingled themselves profusely with the elms and ashes and druidical oaks of England.

America has made contributions far more vast. Who can estimate the amount, or the value, of the augmentation of the commerce of the world, that has resulted from America? Who can imagine to himself what would be the shock to the Eastern Continent, if the Atlantic were no longer traversable or there were no longer American productions or American markets?

But America exercises influences or holds out examples for the consideration of the Old World, of a much higher order, because they are of a moral and political character. America has furnished to Europe, proof of the fact, that popular institutions founded on equality and the principle of representation, are capable of maintaining governments, able to secure the rights of persons, property, and reputation.

America has proved that it is practicable to elevate the mass of mankind—that portion which, in Europe, is called the laboring or lower class; to raise them to self-respect, to make them competent to act a part in the great right and great duty of self-government; and this, she has proved, may be done by the diffusion of knowledge. She holds out an example a thousand times more enchanting, than ever was presented before, to those nine tenths of the human race, who are born without hereditary fortune or hereditary rank.

America has furnished to the world the character of Washington. And if our American institutions had done nothing else, that alone would have entitled them to the respect of mankind. Washington! "First in war, first in peace, and first in the hearts of his countrymen!" Washington is all our own!

The enthusiastic veneration and regard in which the people of the United States hold him, prove them to be worthy of such a countryman, while his reputation abroad reflects the highest honor on his country and its institutions. I would cheerfully put the question to any of the intelligence of Europe and the world: what character of the century, upon the whole, stands out on the relief of history, most pure, most respectable, most sublime? And I doubt not that, by a suffrage approaching to unanimity, the answer would be—Washington!

This structure* by its uprightness, its solidity, its durability is no unfit emblem of his character. His public virtue and public principles were as firm as the earth on which it stands; his personal motives as pure as the serene heaven in which its summit is lost. But, indeed, though a fit, it is an inadequate emblem. Towering high above the column which our hands have builded, beheld not by the inhabitants of a single city, or a single state, ascends the colossal grandeur of his character and his life. In all the constituents of the one, in all the acts of the other, in all its titles to immortal love, admiration, and renown, it is an American production.

Washington is the embodiment and vindication of our trans-Atlantic liberty. Born upon our soil, of parents also born upon it; never, for a moment, having had a sight of the old world; instructed, according to the modes of his time, only in the spare but wholesome elementary knowledge which our institutions provide for the children of the people; growing up beneath and penetrated by, the genuine influence of American society; growing up amid our expanding, but not luxurious civilization; partaking in our great destiny of labor, our long contest with unreclaimed nature and uncivilized man, our agony of glory, the war of independence, our great victory of peace, the formation of the Union, and the establishment of the constitution; he is all, all our own! That crowded and glorious life,

"Where multitudes of virtues passed along,
Each pressing foremost in the mighty throng,
Contending to be seen, then making room
For greater multitudes that were to come;—"

that life was the life of an American citizen.

I claim him for America. In all the perils, in every darkened moment of the state, in the midst of the reproaches of enemies and the misgivings of friends, I turn to that transcendent name for courage and for consolation. To him who denies or doubts whether our fervid liberty can be combined with law, with order, with the security of property, with the pursuits and advancement of happiness; to him who denies that our institutions are capable of producing exaltation of soul and the passion of true glory; to him who denies that we have contributed any to the stock of great lessons and great examples; to all these I reply, by pointing to Washington!

*Bunker Hill Monument

QUESTIONS — 1. For what was America indebted to Europe? 2. According to Webster, what were America's greatest contributions to Europe? 3. Why was Washington a totally American product? 4. Why would an audience of Americans in 1843 be eager to hear an eloquent speaker praise an American hero and American contributions to Europe?

SPELL AND DEFINE — (2) culture, assiduous, germinate; (3) respectable, civilized; (4) luxuries, sustenance; (5) traversable; (6) institution, maintain; (7) competent, hereditary; (9) suffrage; (10) durability.

LESSON LXXIII (73)

The American Eagle—NEAL

NOTE—The United States chose the bald eagle as its national bird in 1792. The bald eagle, which only appears bald because its head is covered with white feathers, lives only in North America. On the Great Seal of the United States, an eagle holds an olive branch in one talon and arrows in the other, symbolizing the country's desire for peace but ability to wage war.

There's a fierce gray bird, with a bending beak,
With an angry eye, and a startling shriek,
That nurses her brood where the cliff flowers blow,
On the precipice top, in perpetual snow;
That sits where the air is shrill and bleak,
On the splintered point of a shivered peak,
Bald headed and stripped, like a vulture torn
In wind and strife; her feathers worn,
And ruffled, and stained, while loose and bright,
Round her serpent neck, that is writhing and bare,
Is a crimson collar of gleaming hair,
Like the crest of a warrior, thinned in fight,
And shorn, and bristling. See her! where
She sits, in the glow of the sun-bright air,
With wing half poised, and talons bleeding,

And kindling eye, as if her prey
Had suddenly been snatched away,
While she was tearing it and feeding.
Above the dark torrent, above the bright stream,
The voice may be heard
Of the thunderer's bird,
Calling out to her god in a clear, wild scream,
As she mounts to his throne, and unfolds in his beam;
While her young are laid out in his rich, red blaze,
And their winglets are fledged in his hottest rays.
Proud bird of the cliff!
where the barren yew springs,
Where the sunshine stays, and the wind harp sings,
She sits, unapproachable, pluming her wings.
She screams! She's away! over hill-top and flood,
Over valley and rock, over mountain and wood,
That bird is abroad in the van of her brood!

'Tis the bird of our banner,
the free bird that braves,
When the battle is there, all the wrath of the waves:
That dips her pinions in the sun's first gush;
Drinks his meridian blaze, his farewell flush;
Sits amid stirring stars, and bends her beak,
Like the slipped falcon, when her piercing shriek
Tells that she stoops upon her cleaving wing,
To drink at some new victim's clear, red spring.
That monarch bird! she slumbers in the night,
Upon the lofty air peak's utmost height;
Or sleeps upon the wing, amid the ray
Of steady, cloudless, everlasting day:
Rides with the thunderer in his blazing march,
And bears his lightnings o'er yon boundless arch;
Soars wheeling through the storm, and screams away,
Where the young pinions of the morning play;
Broods with her arrows in the hurricane;
Bears her green laurel o'er the starry plain,

And sails around the skies, and o'er the rolling deeps,
With still unwearied wing, and eye that never sleeps.

QUESTIONS—Study the habits and traits of character of the
bald eagle as described in this poem. Then write an essay ex-
plaining why you think the United States selected it as a
national symbol.

SPELL AND DEFINE—perpetual, poised, prey, torrent, unapproachable, banner, meridian, falcon, wheeling, hurricane.

LESSON LXXIV (74)

America—S. F. SMITH

NOTE—Written by Samuel F. Smith, a 24 year old Baptist cler-
gyman, our national hymn "America" was first publicly sung in
Boston at a Fourth of July celebration at the Park Street
Church. Oliver Wendall Holmes, a Harvard classmate of Smith,
attributes the genius in "America" to its very first word—
"My." Said Holmes, "That little pronoun did it all . . . that puts
'America' in the hearts of the people. . . ."

My country! 'tis of thee,
Sweet land of liberty,
   Of thee I sing;
Land where my fathers died,
Land of the pilgrims' pride;
From every mountain side,
   Let freedom ring.

My native country! thee,
Land of the noble free,
   Thy name I love:
I love thy rocks and rills,
Thy woods and templed hills;

My heart with rapture thrills,
      Like that above.

Let music swell the breeze,
And ring from all the trees,
      Sweet freedom's song;
Let mortal tongues awake,
Let all that breathe partake,
Let rocks their silence break,
      The sound prolong.

Our fathers' God! to thee,
Author of Liberty!
      To thee we sing;
Long may our land be bright
With freedom's holy light;
Protect us by thy might,
      Great God, our King!

QUESTIONS — 1. What is America's outstanding characteristic that is praised in every stanza? 2. Only the briefest allusions are made to historical facts about the country. What are they? (Stanza one) 3. In stanza three what invitation is given to all? 4. What request is sung to God in stanza four?

LESSON LXXV (75)

The Celestial City—BIBLE

NOTE—Ancient Jerusalem had contained the Temple where the visible presence of God was manifested by the Shekinah. Later, in Jesus Christ "the Word was made flesh, and dwelt among us." John the Revelator here reveals that in the New Jerusalem, the Lamb and "God himself shall be with them" for a reign that will endure "forever and ever."

Revelation 21:1-7

And I saw a new heaven and a new earth: for the first heaven and the first earth were passed away; and there was no more sea. And I, John, saw the Holy City, New Jerusalem, coming down from God out of heaven, prepared as a bride adorned for her husband. And I heard a great voice out of heaven saying, Behold! the tabernacle of God is with men, and he will dwell with them, and they shall be his people, and God himself shall be with them, and be their God. And God shall wipe away all tears from their eyes; and there shall be no more death, neither sorrow, nor crying, neither shall there be any more pain: for the former things are passed away.

And He that sat upon the throne said, Behold! I make all things new. And He said unto me, Write: for these words are true and faithful. And He said unto me, It is done! I am Alpha and Omega, the Beginning and the End. I will give unto him that is athirst of the fountain of the water of life freely. He that overcometh shall inherit all things; and I will be his God, and he shall be my son.

Revelation 21:9-11, 18

And there came unto me one of the seven angels which had the seven vials full of the seven last plagues, and talked with me, saying, Come hither, I will show thee the Bride, the Lamb's wife. And He carried me away in the spirit to a great and high mountain, and showed me that great city, the Holy Jerusalem, descending out of heaven from God, having the glory of God. . . . And the city was of pure gold, like unto clear glass.

Revelation 21:22-27

And I saw no temple therein: for the Lord God Almighty and the Lamb are the temple of it. And the city had no need of the sun, neither of the moon, to shine in it: for the glory of God did lighten it, and the Lamb is the light thereof. And the nations of them which are saved shall walk in the light of it; and the kings of earth do bring their glory and honor into it. And the gates of it shall not be shut at all by day, (for there shall be no night there); and they shall bring the glory and honor of the nations into it. And there shall in nowise enter into it any thing that defileth, neither whatsoever worketh abomination, or maketh a lie: but they which are written in the Lamb's book of life.

Revelation 22:1-5

And He showed me a pure river of water of life, clear as crystal, proceeding out of the throne of God and of the Lamb. In the midst of the street of it, and on either side of the river, was there the tree of life, which bare twelve manner of fruits, and yielded her fruit every month: and the leaves of the tree were for the healing of the nations. And there shall be no

more curse; but the throne of God and of the Lamb
shall be in it; and his servants shall serve him: and
they shall see his face. And there shall be no night
there; and they need no candle, neither light of the
sun; for the Lord giveth them light: and they shall
reign forever and ever.

QUESTIONS — 1. Where does the Holy City come from?
2. Why is there no need for sun or moon in the New Jerusalem?
3. Who is the Lamb? On what do you base your answer? 4. Who
will enter the New Jerusalem? Who will not? 5. What proceeds
from the throne of God and the Lamb? 6. What tree is in the
Holy City? 7. How long will the New Jerusalem endure?